D1191646

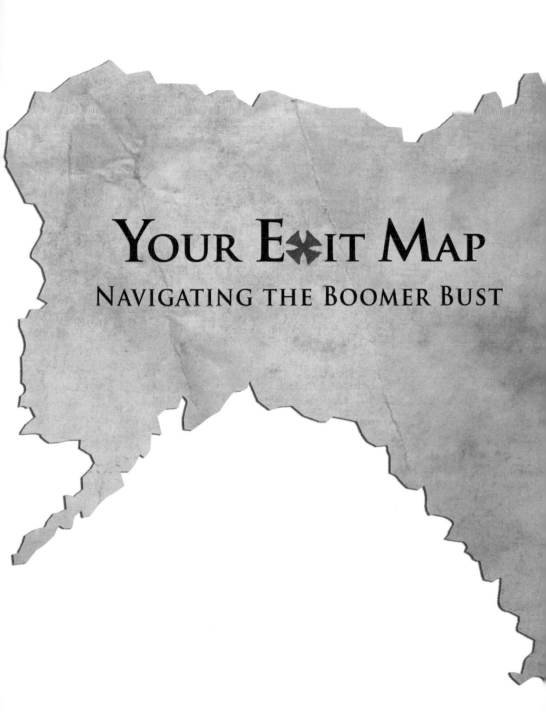

YOUR EXIT MAP

NAVIGATING THE BOOMER BUST

Praise for Your Exit Map

"*Your Exit Map* is an eye opener for any business owner who wonders why he or she should be planning ahead for an exit. Most struggle with the exit phase. This book is a road map for getting it right."

— Gino Wickman, Author of *Traction* and *Rocket Fuel*
Creator of The Entrepreneurial Operating System (EOS)

"Your Exit Map is a fantastic and necessary read for anyone who is looking to sell their business successfully. It is full of great content that will no doubt be valuable to anyone who is either in the process of selling their business, or considering their exit strategy. So I guess that means this is a critical book for any business owner. John Dini has demonstrated great value in his previous books, and this one is no exception."

— Jason P. Zickerman, President & CEO,
The Alternative Board International

"Damn! Just when I thought I couldn't be more impressed with John Dini, he delivers another soon-to-be-award-winning book. Your Exit Map captures the current state of affairs of a unique moment in time: the journey of divestiture by the largest generation of business owners – Baby Boomers – in the history of business ownership on planet Earth.

John tells this story using words, pictures and graphics – lots of color – that manifest as wisdom, perspective, and even fun. If you're one of these Boomer business owners, John shows you how you can make this journey, including identifying tips, best practices and people who can help you with the navigation.

— Jim Blasingame, Host of *The Small Business Advocate® Show*
Author of *The Age of the Customer*

"*Your Exit Map* is on the money as it weighs in on the impact of the largest entrepreneurial generation in history, how they drove economic expansion, and how their leaving the workplace will create financial ripples throughout the economy.

— Don Douglas, Janitor, Liquid Networx

"If you are a boomer and business owner, the adage 'fail to plan, plan to fail,' is painfully evident throughout this book. Fortunately the keys to making the right deal for the right reasons – and at the right time – are laid out in straightforward terms."

— Doug Kisgen, Speaker, Growth Producer, Turnover Fixer
Author of *Rethink Happy*

"*Your Exit Map* combines entertainment with deep industry knowledge. A wealth of illustrations add both clarity and humor to business concepts that are sometimes difficult to fully absorb. In addition, the accompanying website provides even more value with its interactive tools and educational resources.

John F. Dini has delivered an exit planning book that is different, informative and unusually fun reading. If you are only going to read one book about planning your transition from a business, Your Exit Map should be it."

— Wendy Keller, Publishing Strategist and
Author of *The Ultimate Guide to Platform Building*,
Secrets of Successful Negotiation and other titles

"I am actively involved in several national accounting associations, and the vast number of retiring Baby Boomers is being discussed with increasing urgency. *Your Exit Map* gives both owners and their advisors a clear and entertaining look at why preparation is vital and how to begin the process."

— John Wright, Marketing Managing Partner,
Austin & San Antonio, RSM US LLP

"Working with thousands of entrepreneurs, I can tell you the coming crisis is REAL. The Exit Map is a timely and needed call to action for business owners everywhere to play offense before reality puts you in a costly defensive position around stewarding what is typically your greatest legacy asset."

— Mike Sharrow, President & CEO, The C12 Group

"*Your Exit Map* is an eye opening look at the effect of the largest entrepreneurial generation in history as they leave the workplace. It's a must read for any business owner who wonders why he or she should be planning ahead for an exit."

— Donald L. Mooney, CEO, Donald L. Mooney Enterprises
2015 Veteran Minority Firm of the Year

"Exit strategy planning can be tough and lonely work. Most business owners don't know where to turn or how to start. John Dini's practical guide to exiting a business can help any business owner to regain some control over one of the most confusing and challenging times in an entrepreneur's career.

Along with a host of user-friendly tools on the Exit Map website, the book provides a step-by-step process that any business owner can use to make key decisions, plot a new path and execute a plan that meets his or her needs. Once again, John has combined his wealth of experience with his talent for telling the story!"

— Lisë Stewart, Executive Director,
Galliard Family Business Advisor Institute

"*Your Exit Map* delivers solid advice on planning a transition from your company in an informative and entertaining manner. It is full of tidbits about Boomers (the largest entrepreneurial generation in U.S. history) and their businesses that made a significant and prolonged impact on our economy."

— James D. Goudge, Chairman, Broadway Bank

"John Dini continues to blend the art and the science of exit planning into brilliant intellectual property. John brings the science that doesn't change (example: we are all going to leave our business) into an artful understanding that simplifies this chaotic mess."

— Larry Linne, CEO, InCite Performance Group
Author of *Make the Noise Go Away*

"Dini's book provides a clear and brilliant roadmap to leverage all the hard work that owners put in over the years into an optimal outcome. It spells out what is required to maximize success, step by step. A so needed resource at the perfect time. You won't find better guidance anywhere else."

— Andre Berger, MD, Chief Executive Officer National ACO, LLC

"I believe you have captured their story and its impact on the world. Your planning and transition advice to the Baby Boomer business owner is excellent and straight forward."

— Ed Lette, CEO, Business Bank of Texas

"*Your Exit Map* is a fascinating quick read combining storytelling, history and the cold, hard facts of what every baby boomer business owner (and their advisors) is facing in the months and years ahead. Anyone who is, or is related to a business owner, should give this a read."

— Paul Cronin, Partner and Director of Business Development, Successful Transition Planning Institute

"*Your Exit Map* is a stunning look at the effect of the Baby Boomer tidal wave, and the impact of their retirement from entrepreneurship. If you are wondering when, how or why you should plan ahead for your transition, the answers are here."

— Kevin Short, Managing Partner & CEO, Clayton Capital Partners
Author of *Sell Your Business for an Outrageous Price*

"Dini has done it again! In *Your Exit Map*, John, a longtime, skilled and Certified Exit Planner™, goes beyond describing the challenges Boomer owners face as they exit their companies. Dini shows owners how to meet those challenges and remain in control no matter what type of successor they choose."

— John H. Brown, Founder, Business Enterprise Institute
Author of *Exit Planning: The Definitive Guide*

Also by John F. Dini

11 Things You Absolutely Need to Know About Selling Your Business

Hunting in a Farmer's World

A guide to selling your business
in a highly competitive market

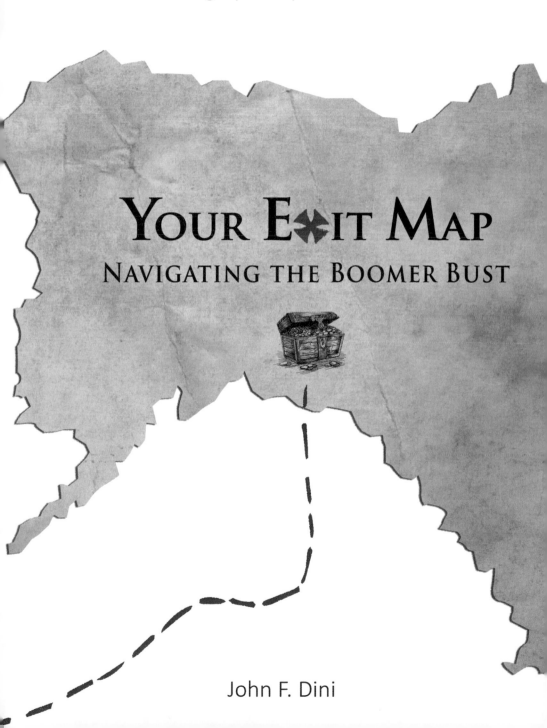

YOUR EXIT MAP

NAVIGATING THE BOOMER BUST

John F. Dini

Printed in the United States of America
Library of Congress Control Number: 2017930093

ISBN-10: 0-9790531-4-5
ISBN-13: 978-0-9790531-4-6

First Printing: May 2017
10 9 8 7 6 5 4 3 2

Introduction

This book is the culmination of ten years of research, writing and speaking about the impending exodus of the Baby Boomers from business ownership. They are the wealthiest, and perhaps the hardest working generation in American history. They own more businesses, both in gross numbers and as a percentage of the population, than any generation before or since.

At every stage of their lives, as consumers and workers, Boomers have created one-time distortions of historical trends. As they leave the workplace, they will do it again.

In 2007 a colleague in the business brokerage industry came to me. He had just read *The $10 Trillion Opportunity,* by Richard E. Jackim and Peter G. Christman. In the book the authors described how the transfer of Baby Boomer assets would provide a multi-decade windfall for business brokers, financial managers and estate planners everywhere. As business brokers, he felt our streets were about to become paved in gold, and we couldn't possibly miss making a very large amount of money.

My many years of experience as a business owner have taught me to be very, very skeptical whenever someone says a proposition "can't miss." As a broker, I knew that every successful transaction required not only a seller but a complementary buyer as well. I began digging a little deeper into what kind of buyers we might expect to have on the receiving end of all these upcoming business transitions.

What I found was not only enlightening; it was startling.

By the end of that year I had summarized my research into an article titled "The Boomer Bust?" for the local business journal. That led to an invitation to be a luncheon speaker at a seminar on selling companies, sponsored by a business brokerage and a law firm. It was my first "Beating the Boomer Bust" presentation. Over the last 10 years I've given versions of that presentation to thousands of business owners and their advisors around the country.

In 2010 I serialized much of what I had learned in eight consecutive weekly installments for my online column **www.awakeat2oclock.com**. With some editing and typesetting, that became the e-book, *Beating the Boomer Bust: How Baby Boomers changed the face of small business in America, and why it isn't over yet.* It summarized my findings and predictions about the impact that retiring Baby Boomers would have on small business in America in about 50 pages.

At about the same time I decided to discontinue my business brokerage activities and began studying to become a Certified Exit Planner. By the end of 2010, I was designing exit strategies for business owners who were still 3 to 10 years away from retirement.

In 2015 I began exiting my peer advisory and coaching business so I could concentrate on exit planning full-time. We also started designing an assessment tool for owners who wanted to know how prepared they were to enter an exit planning process. That tool is now available, along with a lot of other free resources, at **www.YourExitMap.com**.

Finally, my friends and associates began asking when I was going to write "the book."

I have two other published books to my credit. *11 Things You Absolutely Need To Know about Selling Your Business* (second edition) is a simple guide for smaller or "Main Street" owners who are seeking to sell their business to a third-party.

My 2014 book *Hunting in a Farmers World: Celebrating the Mind of an Entrepreneur* has won numerous business book awards. It provides a deeper look into the psychology of a business owner from the startup of a business through their final exit.

Despite having written tens of thousands of words about the transition of the Baby Boomers from their businesses, and spoken hundreds of thousands of words to audiences on the topic, I never actually put everything down in one place.

This is that book. I know that you will enjoy it; and I think you will find it eye opening as well.

Contents

Author's Note

Beating the Boomer Bust, whether experienced as a presentation, the original e-book, or in my articles over the years, has often been characterized as "remarkably enlightening but also somewhat depressing."

The purpose of this book is to inform business owners of a strategic issue that *WILL* affect their businesses and their lives after their businesses. Most are unaware of its size and scope. For that reason, I took great pains in providing the statistics and calculations that support my conclusions.

For almost ten years I've been acting as a kind of "Paul Revere;" warning about the Boomer Surge of transitions. If you read this book, you'll understand why I believe it is inevitable. My conclusions are my own, but the numbers are real.

Please note that I don't sell products related to my predictions. I don't pitch gold futures or stock market advice. I am an exit planner; but this isn't an advertisement for my exit planning practice. I couldn't begin to handle a fraction of one percent of what's coming, even if I dedicated the rest of my life to it.

This book is for the millions of hard working entrepreneurs who don't deserve to be blindsided.

Acknowledgements

First and always, to my wife Leila. She is the rock, the manager, the tracker of details, and the one who makes sure the bills get paid when I go off on projects like this one.

I can't say enough about the team. This is our second book together, and it's been even more fun than the last one.

Christi Brendlinger, who considers "Too bad we couldn't..." to be her marching orders. Christi is my editor, when she isn't creating the web tools or building a new site, or managing the actual publication of the book.

Sarah Salgado. The "glue" who maintains communications between the four of us on the book team, because she is the only one who knows what everyone is working on. Also quite simply the best. proofreader.ever.

And Beth Sorenson of BNS Mission Design. Her dogged determination to find the right picture or create the right graphic to illustrate a point was amazing. Her humor and keen eye is apparent on every page, and really made this a collaboration where the whole is greater than the sum of the parts.

Thanks also to Don Douglas, who told me to stop fooling around and write the book. To Agnes Mura, my business coach, and Wendy Keller of Keller Media, my marketing coach, for their patience and insight.

Finally, to all the entrepreneurs in this book, previous books and books yet to come. Without your inspiring stories and willingness to help others, none of this would be possible.

Style Note

I am not gender biased, but writing around politically correct usage of both male and female pronouns gets old, and disrupts the rhythm of a sentence. I refer to both where it seems appropriate, but more often default to the male pronoun for better flow. Most of the successful female entrepreneurs that I know understand that they work in a male dominated business environment, and shrug it off. I have no intention of slighting or demeaning female owners. A hunter is a hunter.

Thank You Critical Readers

Many thanks to the folks who volunteered to read excerpts, provide feedback and suggest additions to the content. Larry Amon, Steven Bankler, Jack Beacham, Mike Beldon, Richard A. Bufalini, Mark Crossman, Wynesta Dale, Mike Derosa, Tom Dooley, Gary Doxstater, David Fox, Rob Fricker, Christopher George, Arnold Goldman, David Granato, Eric Gustafson, Mike Havel, John Hill, Trip Holmes, Nancy Hyde, Ellwood Jones, Bob Kroon, Nancy Kudla, Jerry Lawson, Steve Leach, Tom Majcher, Jim Marshall, Buzz Miller, Tali Nizic, Mark Nonweiler, Edward Rosenberg, Jim Sandler, Michael Schanzer, Keith Schellin, Jim Stauder, Alfonso Tomita, Peter Vadas, Oswald Viva, Mike Warmington, Mike Weaver, Dave Weinkauf, and William Young.

PART ONE

The Unstoppable Force
that is the Baby Boom

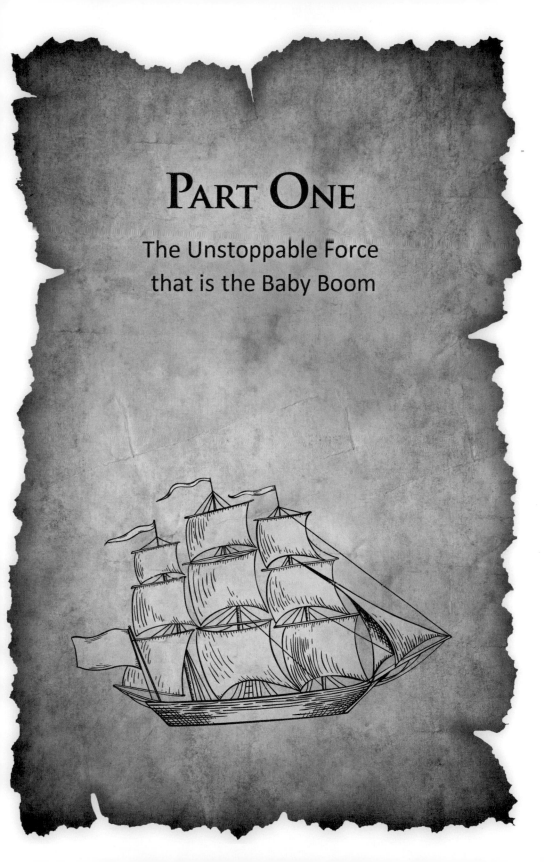

1.1 The Tsunami

Peter Drucker is often called "the founder of modern management." He once said, *"I don't predict the future. I look at what has happened already and point out the inevitable result."* I've been speaking and writing for over a decade about the inevitable results of the Baby Boomer Tsunami.

Winston Churchill said, *"Those that don't understand history are doomed to repeat it."* While we will never repeat the scale of the Baby Boom, understanding its impact is still vital. It's difficult to accept the scope and depth of what is happening today, and what will be happening for the next 20 years, without studying what has happened already.

The first half of this book looks at what made the Baby Boom generation the force that it was and still is. If you are a Boomer, you'll probably enjoy some of the nostalgia. If you are younger, you are likely already tired of hearing about the Boomers. Nonetheless, comprehending their unique impact on business, and why they were honed into competitive entrepreneurs during a time of plenty in America, is a prerequisite for successfully navigating the storm that is coming.

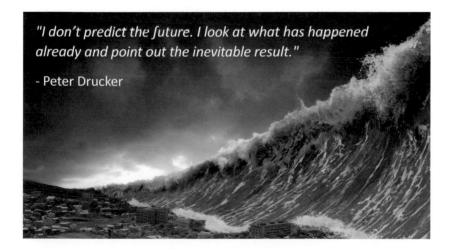

"I don't predict the future. I look at what has happened already and point out the inevitable result."

- Peter Drucker

In 1945, GIs returning from World War II began to marry and start families at an astounding rate. America had conquered two totalitarian empires and made the world safe for democracy. The future was bright. The cost of living was relatively low in comparison to wages, and in the U.S. the middle class was expanding rapidly.

Young parents honestly believed that their children could grow up to be anything; from a lawyer or a physician to the President of the United States. From 1945 to 1946 the birthrate exploded from 2.8 million to 3.5 million, an astonishing 24% increase in just one year. By 1954, it had grown another 15% annually to 4 million, and then peaked at 4.3 million in 1957. That was a mind-boggling 68% increase in births from just 12 years before.

The curve of the Baby Boomer birthrate became the template for many statistical charts over the next 40 years. Shifts in social

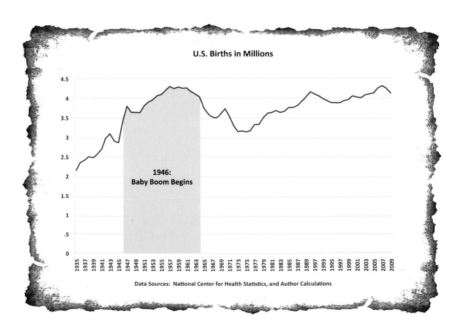

U.S. Births in Millions

1946: Baby Boom Begins

Data Sources: National Center for Health Statistics, and Author Calculations

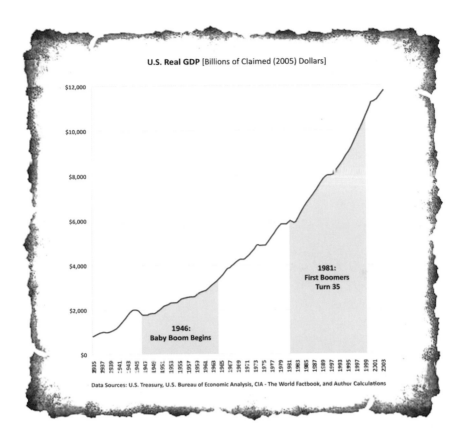

U.S. Real GDP [Billions of Claimed (2005) Dollars]

1981:
First Boomers
Turn 35

1946:
Baby Boom Begins

Data Sources: U.S. Treasury, U.S. Bureau of Economic Analysis, CIA - The World Factbook, and Author Calculations

attitudes, including those involving civil rights, women's roles in the family, college educations, divorce and marriage began accelerating in the mid-1960s as the majority of Boomers reached their 20s.

The U.S. economy experienced 40 years of sustained growth as a result of the influx of new workers and consumers. Products and services designed specifically for Boomers became overnight phenomenon.

Marketers who understood how to approach and appeal to Boomers as children, teens and young adults, and later as parents, had a guaranteed formula for success.

As Boomers reached their 30s, they formed businesses at a rate and in numbers that eclipses anything done by previous or following generations. We will discuss the reasons for that as we progress, but right now suffice to say that Boomers as a demographic group are 2.5 times more likely to own their own business than those of any other generation.

As Boomers in their 40s and 50s amassed collective wealth unimaginable to future generations, conspicuous consumption drove the markets in everything from McMansions to luxury automobiles through the 1980s and 1990s.

Today, the business world is preparing for the Boomers' retirements. Once again marketers are reaching out to the wealthiest (and most free spending) generation in history. From independent living centers to bathrooms with walk in tubs, and from self-driving cars to stand up bicycles, businesses that offer products designed specifically for Boomers continue to thrive. Boomers are accustomed to living in a world designed with their needs and comfort in mind.

1.2 The Multiplier Effect: Television

The sheer number of Baby Boomers would be influential all by itself. By 1965, 40% of the United States population, two out of every five people, were under the age of 21. Even 78 million children, however, isn't a historically high number as a percentage. What made the Baby Boomers such a powerful force was their commonality.

By 1965, 40% of the U.S. population
was under the age of 21.

Prior to World War II mass media was just beginning to have an impact. The only real news outlets worthy of that description were the young radio networks and national magazines. The radio networks focused on syndicated entertainment, while news programs were still overwhelmingly local. National magazines such as *Life* and *Look* impacted millions with their photo essays, but such publications as a whole were still designed for general consumption; tailored for adult readers.

That changed overnight with the introduction of television. The first television stations started broadcasting in the late 1930s. The demonstration of TV was a huge hit at the 1939 World's Fair in New York. Even so, general TV manufacturing came to a stop with the onset of World War II. After the war, returning GIs were anxious to spend on consumer goods, and factories built for wartime electronics production were more than ready to deliver.

MODEL HM-225

A strikingly attractive 22-tube Television Receiver with both picture and sound reception. Picture size 5 ¾ by 7 ¾ inches. 5 Television Channels. Touch Tuning Selector Keys. 12-inch Dynapower Speaker. 10 Watts Output.

In 1948, the first television networks, CBS and NBC, began broadcasting syndicated content nationally. In 1951, color televisions were introduced. The first Boomers were just 6 years old.

**Check out the Baby Boomer Fun Facts
at www.YourExitMap.com.**

Unlike almost every other country, the United States developed television as private enterprise rather than a government monopoly. Following the model of the radio networks, content was paid for by commercial advertising. In fact, many of the consumer brands that made radio successful were the very first to move headlong into the new medium.

As television quickly assimilated into the average middle-class American home, viewers were identified with a new name, consumers. Programming was designed to target specific "audience segments." Daytime television was developed for stay-at-home mothers, with a wealth of soap operas supported by health, beauty and household convenience advertising.

Evening programming, dominated by a steady diet of westerns and police procedurals, was targeted to fathers returning from work. Primetime, starting at 7:00 in each time zone, allowed enough time for the patriarch of the family to leave work at 5:00 and eat dinner with the family, before settling down for a night in front of the TV set.

It didn't take very long for Madison Avenue to realize that 40% of their potential audience was children. Afternoons, when school classes were over and mothers were busy preparing dinner, were reserved for programming targeted to children. For the first time ever, children were regarded as a consumer group separate and distinct from their parents.

Prior to television, children were raised in anticipation of their adult life being a duplicate of that of their parents'. Sons were encouraged to follow in their father's career footsteps. Daughters were expected to marry and raise children. Middle-class families, enjoying a consumer lifestyle beyond what most of their Depression-era parents dreamed, relocated to the suburbs, but not very far from the region where they were born. If they owned an automobile, travel was still mostly limited to day trips from home.

Like many early Boomers, I was raised in a culture that was defined by regional and ethnic dominance. Children had for generations grown up with roughly the same attitudes, the same ideas, and the same habits as their parents. They just hadn't experienced much else.

I grew up in the industrial middle Atlantic Northeast. "Ethnicity" in my world meant Polish, Italian, German or Irish. Of course we had discrimination, bigotry and ghettos. I cringe at some of the racist nursery rhymes I was taught by my friends as a child. But we didn't have Jim Crow laws, or poll tests, and although my schools were largely white, it was as a result of the neighborhood, not of the law.

Boomer children
became a consumer class.

I had no idea what rhubarb or okra were until I was an adult. I had never heard of ice fishing. Iced tea came in one flavor; if you wanted "sweet tea" you put sugar in. When I was 20 or so, I remember reading a debate in a restaurant industry magazine about whether America was ready to accept a regional ethnic food into the mainstream... pizza! My neighborhood had a family-owned pizza parlor on virtually every corner. It shocked me to realize that everyone else's didn't.

This regionalism was eradicated during the last years of the Baby Boom in the mid-1960s. GIs who had been stationed in other parts of the country during the war, especially California, picked up their wives and children and moved in search of greater opportunity. National brands dominated household goods, powered by the reach of television advertising. News was nationwide. Boomers

grew up seeing the same national news stories (with the same editorial slant) regardless of where they lived.

Boomer children had become a consumer class, and for the first time products and their associated marketing, were designed specifically for them. Whether they realized it or not, they were paid far more attention as a demographic segment than any generation before.

Walt Disney was a genius in his early recognition of the power of television. In 1955, Disney opened Disneyland in Anaheim, California and simultaneously launched "The Mickey Mouse Club" on national television. The television show was built around the primary cartoon character in the Disney film stable, interspersed with travelogues about the joy of visiting his eponymous theme park. The Mouseketeers were carefully modeled as kids "just like me." (Albeit all white and carefully supervised by smiling men.)

Disney's brilliance lay in his realization that children could influence consumer decisions, and no longer relied solely on their parents to decide every purchase. They could identify and ask for products that their parents were previously unaware of, because they had seen them on TV.

This is one of the earliest examples of the purchasing power of the Baby Boomers.

From the late 1950s through the first few years of the 1960s, at the height of The Mickey Mouse Club's popularity, Mouseketeer ears became a reasonably inexpensive "must-have" for preteens. They were the first Boomer driven product hit, to be followed by Silly Putty, Hula Hoops, and scores of other advertising-driven fads.

Pause for a moment to consider the sales process for proprietary products in the 1950s. While Mouseketeer ears were available at some department stores, there were no specialty chains catering to children such as Toys"R"Us, much less branded stores such as Disney has today. Mouseketeer ears were available chiefly by mail order.

Mail order sales were exactly what the title indicates. You didn't order by telephone and receive it by mail; you ordered by mail and then the products were sent back by mail. There were no 800 numbers. Long-distance calling was prohibitively expensive and not very reliable. There were no charge cards. (Diners Club, a cardboard discount membership card, was introduced in 1950 and didn't become a plastic "credit card" until 1961.) Of course, there certainly was no Internet.

So apart from those who lived in large cities with access to national department store chains, the majority of Americans had to order their children's Mouseketeer ears by mail. They filled out a request by hand, placed cash, a check or postage stamps (which were still legally acceptable as currency) in an envelope and mailed the order to Anaheim, California.

Despite what we would today consider insurmountable odds against selling a product, from 1957 until about 1963 the Disney Company steadily shipped *25,000 pairs of Mouseketeer ears a DAY*. The Boomers had established themselves as a buying force, and Madison Avenue quickly took notice.

From 1957 to 1963, Disney shipped
25,000 pairs of Mouseketeer ears a DAY.

In 1946, Dr. Benjamin Spock authored *The Common Sense Book of Baby and Child Care*. It was a huge hit, selling 500,000 copies in the first six months after publication. It became the Bible of child rearing in the United States; an apt description since it was outsold by only the Bible in the entire 20th century.

Parents who raised "Spock Babies" reversed previously accepted norms of pediatric care. Before the book was published, children's schedules were closely controlled, and training in activities of daily living took place at specific ages. Spock's book argued that a parent should first see to the emotional needs of their child, and be flexible in designing their parenting around the child's wishes and a more individual development schedule.

You can download cool Boomer infographics
at www.YourExitMap.com

Child raising in the family started to evolve from "children should be seen and not heard," to making the kids the center of attention. Family activities revolved around youth sports and school pageants. Keeping up with the Joneses became keeping up with the Joneses' kids. The first Little League team outside Pennsylvania was formed in 1947, and by 1955, just seven years later, there were organized Little Leagues in all 48 states. Newly middle-class parents were determined that their children would have an appropriate slice of the American Dream.

Even as parents were catering to their children's individualism, toy manufacturers were expanding it to new levels. In 1959, Mattel Corporation launched what may have been the most influential toy in history, Barbie. The first Boomer girls were fourteen years old.

Prior to Barbie, all dolls (except some collectables) were baby dolls. They existed principally to train little girls in the virtues of motherhood. Dolls could be dressed, diapered and fed. Accessories were chiefly strollers and little cradles.

Barbie changed little girls' fantasy play forever. Although she started out as a young housewife with a dream home, Barbie's career possibilities soon grew. By 1963, she was a corporate executive, long before the term "glass ceiling" was coined. In 1965, Barbie became an Astronaut, four years before Neil Armstrong went to the moon.

Barbie not only enabled girls to see themselves in new roles, she brought them further than they had previously imagined. (By the early 1990's she was a Presidential candidate, 25 years prior to the candidacy of Hillary Clinton.) Notably however, of the 150 official versions of Barbie from race car driver to rock star, there is one that is missing.

There is no Mommy Barbie. There are no Baby Barbies. Boomer girls grew into Boomer women with an entirely different agenda than those who preceded them, and Barbie was a contributing factor in their development.

Thanks to the revenue provided by advertisers chasing a massive new market, television was the medium that ensured the majority of 78 million Baby Boomers experienced the same events, received the same news, and enjoyed the same fads simultaneously. Not only were they 40% of the population, they were also the first demographic group to go through each stage of life collectively, and they did it with greater impact than anyone had seen before.

They made up the single most powerful interest group in history. And the Boomers chief interest, enthusiastically supported by experts and parents and products and advertisers all around them, was themselves.

1.3 The Economic Mother Load

The impact of 78 million children on the economy was startling, but it was only a foreshadowing of what was to come. Boomers reached adulthood with an expectation that the world would pay attention to them, but once they arrived at working age they found that growing up as the center of attention didn't automatically ensure success.

Boomers were raised to expect success. I heard, "You can be anything you want to be when you grow up," around the dinner table frequently, as I expect most other middle-class Boomers did as well. That success, while expected, was anything but assured.

Boomers were raised to expect success.

Boomer children were already experiencing a scarcity of resources by the time they reached elementary school. Public school classrooms frequently held 40 or 50 students, and in some parochial schools I attended, 70 children in a class was not unheard of. There simply were not enough classrooms or teachers to handle the demand.

Many of us remember double sessions, where the student body was split into morning and afternoon class schedules to allow twice the utilization of the classrooms (and the teachers). I spoke to one woman from New York City who recalls growing up with triple sessions. Students were divided into morning, midday, and late afternoon sessions so that no more than two thirds of the students were present at any one time.

The economic theory of the velocity of money examines how many times an amount changes hands in a series of transactions. The impact of the Boomer Surge on school enrollments is but one place to examine that effect. Families of increasing size and wealth flocked to the suburbs to buy tract homes in formerly agricultural areas and built an entire social system around their kids.

Fortunately, the burgeoning property taxes that resulted from this migration provided much needed funds that could be channeled into more schools. Construction jobs, teachers, administrators, school lunch ladies, textbook printers, bus manufacturers, and city employment grew by leaps and bounds. Keeping up was difficult, but robust economic growth made it easier.

The addition of consumers into an economy is the rising tide that lifts all boats. The impact is undeniable, and the opposite is equally true. A reduction in consumers is a terrible thing for any economy. As an example, the Black Death of the mid-1300s in Europe is estimated to have killed almost half of the population. Europe's economy did not fully recover for almost 300 years. Imagine going for *generations* without any need for new housing or manufacturing capability.

We can easily identify modern examples in the economies of Europe. The "weak sisters" of the European Union, Portugal, Italy, Greece and Spain (collectively the PIGS) share one notable trait in common. They rank as the countries with the four lowest birth rates in the European Union over the last 30 years. Fiscal mismanagement certainly plays a part in their current troubles, but the underlying weakness in their economies stems from a lack of new workers and a decline in the number of new consumers.

Fewer children means fewer consumers, and eventually fewer workers to produce for those consumers. We'll see later in this book how the trend of declining birth rates has affected the United States and why the increase of birthrates with the Millennials offers promise for the future, although perhaps not in time for Baby Boomer business owners.

Boomer children had to compete for attention in crowded classrooms, and when they reached college age the situation only got worse. The rate of college-educated workers as a percentage of total population in America had held steady at around 6% for several generations, but that was about to change dramatically.

Boomers tripled the number of college-educated employees in the workforce.

Once again, the sheer number of Boomers determined to get what they wanted in life proved to be an indomitable force. The higher education infrastructure had no chance, and was totally overwhelmed by the influx of applicants.

From 1967 (beginning when the first Boomers turned 21) through 1976, the number of graduates from American colleges with four-year degrees increased from just over 500,000 to 1 million *annually.*

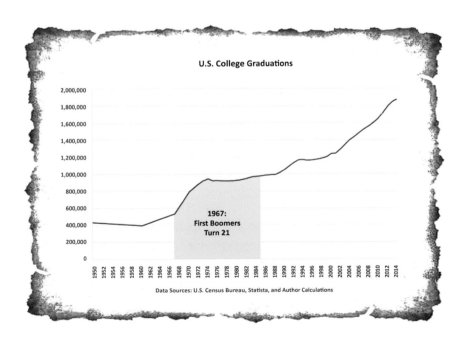

U.S. College Graduations

1967: First Boomers Turn 21

Data Sources: U.S. Census Bureau, Statista, and Author Calculations

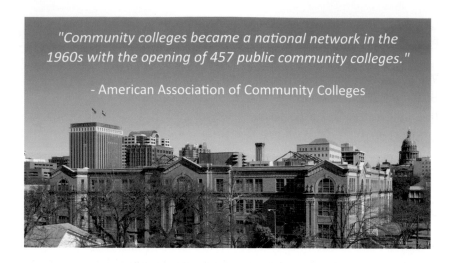

> *"Community colleges became a national network in the 1960s with the opening of 457 public community colleges."*
>
> - American Association of Community Colleges

In raw numbers that's an increase in the 20 years the Boomers went to college, from just over 8 million college graduates in the workforce to about 28 million, a 300% leap. This doesn't even count the two-year degrees conferred by over 400 community colleges that opened in the 1960s to handle the overflow.

A college education became the ticket to the American Dream. Even so, there were millions of degreed people for whom there simply wasn't enough space, regardless of their qualifications. For every available job, there were scores of applicants. Corporate America struggled to absorb even the best.

In a single generation the average number of college-educated workers in the U.S. workforce rose from 6% to 24%, or approximately the same percentage as today, some 40 years later. This is a

> *"What Americans have to understand is that this country reached its demographic peak 10 years ago."*
>
> - David T Beers, Director of Standard & Poor's Sovereign Credit Rating unit on the downgrading of America's debt from AAA to AA+.

phenomenon that occurs repeatedly with these "Pig in a Python" Boomer driven surges.

Whether it's the economy, social structures or politics; the Boomers account for a tectonic one-time shift that has remained flat afterwards, despite the growing population of the country. It's another critical component to consider when discussing the future of Boomer-owned businesses.

1.4 The Speed of Change

When we were teenagers, the world seemed to change rapidly around us. As the Boomers reached their teens, the speed of change affected their entire universe.

In 1964, the United States Congress legalized "The Pill" for oral contraception. Freed from the threat of unwanted pregnancies and shotgun marriages, the Boomers became the "Free Love" generation.

The speed of change
affected the Baby Boomer's entire universe.

Marijuana use, the high of choice for the Beat Generation, spread rapidly. Fueled by popular books by Carlos Castaneda (*The Teachings of Don Juan* – 1968) and Tom Wolfe (*The Electric Kool-Aid Acid Test* – 1968) the Boomers' search for expanded consciousness went mainstream.

The speed of change was exponential and evident everywhere in popular culture. It's hard to believe in retrospect but only five years passed between the 1964 Ed Sullivan show featuring the radically-haircut Beatles and the 500,000 "hippies" partying down at Max Yasgur's farm in Woodstock, New York.

The time span from the cancellation of *Leave It to Beaver's* separate marriage bed family sitcom (1963) to *Star Trek* seeking out new civilizations in space (1966) was only three years. *The Mod Squad* with their three hip co-stars (a black man, a woman and a hip white guy) premiered two years later. The advertising industry knew who their prime audience was, and demanded that the networks deliver programming to meet their tastes.

In short order, TV presented the first African-American character in a series (Bill Cosby in *I Spy* – 1965) and variety host (*The Flip Wilson Show* – 1970). Social/political satire went prime time with *The Smothers Brothers' Comedy Hour* in 1967 and *All in The Family* in 1971. What the Boomers wanted to watch, the nation watched.

With anti-war protests, women's liberation, environmental activism, a lowered voting age, civil rights, pop art, rock and roll, and the landing on the Moon, Boomers grappled with change. They were living in a day-by-day dynamically changing world and thanks to mass media, everyone was included whether they liked it or not.

From elementary school drills for nuclear attacks, (was hiding under the desk really going to help?) to three shocking assassinations and the Cuban Missile Crisis, Boomers were acutely aware that the secure, Ozzie-and-Harriet world they enjoyed as children was gone forever.

Boomers created change, accepted change, and came to expect change. If their world wasn't what they wanted or envisioned, it was their prerogative to make it different.

1.5 "I am what I do."

It is certainly easier to predict the future when we can see the trends of 30 or 40 years compacted into a few thousand words. It wasn't as easily understood by the bright-eyed college graduates who in the 1970s planned to embark on professional careers.

Many Boomers discovered that a college degree did not guarantee prosperity.

As these new workers began pouring into the economy they once again found that the world was unprepared to receive them. Corporate America could not create three times the number of fast-track management jobs that existed in the 1950s and 1960s. Many Boomers came out of college and found that they had hit a brick wall in their pursuit of prosperity.

In the recession of 1973 to 1975, the longest recession between World War II and the Great Recession of 2007 to 2009, talented twenty-something Boomers found themselves in many positions

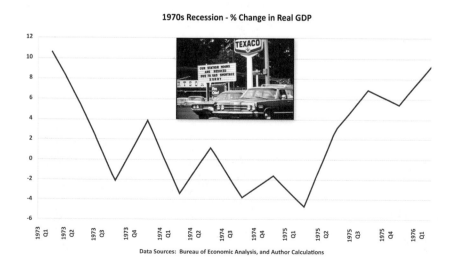

1970s Recession - % Change in Real GDP

Data Sources: Bureau of Economic Analysis, and Author Calculations for which they were overqualified. During that time I worked in a warehouse in New Jersey. Although I personally was only halfway to my bachelor's degree, my five man loading dock crew included a history teacher, a marine biologist and an engineer.

Not one of us was resigned to a new career path. We all knew without a doubt that we would resume our upward track as soon as we could get a foothold. As Boomers, we grew up expecting it as our birthright.

This competition for upward mobility that matches their expectations is one of the distinctive traits that drive Boomers. Surrounded by equally qualified candidates, the only way to stand out was by outperforming your peers. From the mid-1970s to the mid-1990s, when the Baby Boomers were in their 30s and 40s, the average workweek for white-collar employees went from just over 40 hours to almost 54 hours a week. The race was on, and Boomers were determined to win.

Interviews with Influencers

Tom James

Tom James is the Executive Chairman of Raymond James Financial, Inc. (www.raymondjames.com) and its subsidiary, Raymond James & Associates Inc. He was the Chief Executive Officer of the Company for 40 years until relinquishing the role in 2010. The company has over 7,000 financial advisors serving nearly 3,000,000 client accounts with over half a trillion dollars in assets.

"I started out driving through neighborhoods, and getting out of my car to chat with people. Those days are no longer. That said, we also have to be on the front lines of the virtual world."

I wanted to do something well that many CEOs do poorly, accomplish a planned succession while I was still working. I stepped down as CEO after 40 years, and then as Chairman after another six. I still work full time, but my focus now is preparing the institution for success in future generations. My principal role is as the steward of our culture.

We are actively teaming older financial advisor employees and independent contractors with younger ones, so that as they reach the end of their career, they have a book of business to sell to an identified buyer. Their accounts don't revert to the company.

Younger workers need more help in socializing. This is a face to face business, and they will have to assume greater roles in the community. Good works are a part of who we are, and they help our younger people get involved with prospective clients as they both help less fortunate members of the community.

I began by driving through neighborhoods, and getting out of my car to chat with people. Those days are no longer. That said, we also have to be on the front lines of the virtual world. Raymond James budgeted $275,000,000 this year for information technology, but high-tech only facilitates relationships.

We are experiencing the lowest fee levels in our industry's history, while being saddled with Government-imposed costs that are becoming ridiculous. If we ran our business like the government, we'd be out of business!

There are more similarities between the generations than differences. Both spouses share family and financial responsibility now. Having watched three generations of managers at this company, as well as our clients, I can say that they all worry about the same things over time.

Boomers grew up believing
an upwardly mobile lifestyle was their birthright.

In their quest for success, Boomers began modifying their family structures. College educated women, raised with Barbie fantasies, had little interest in staying home. Adding a second wage earner to household income was by far the fastest way to accumulate wealth.

This chart again shows the one-time Boomer Surge. Between 1970, when the oldest Boomers turned 25, and 1990, when the youngest reached the same age, the percentage of dual income households more than doubled. As with the other trends, this one levels off after the surge, and has remained virtually flat in the 25 years since. During that time, women entered the workforce at a rate of 1,000,000 annually. Between 1970 and 1980, the

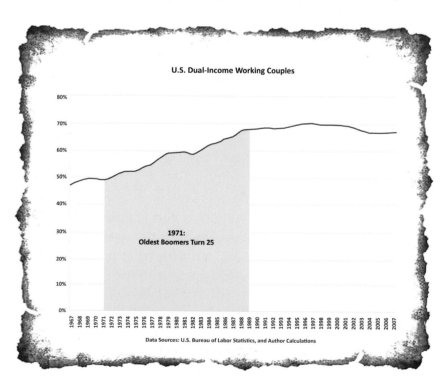

U.S. Dual-Income Working Couples

1971:
Oldest Boomers Turn 25

Data Sources: U.S. Bureau of Labor Statistics, and Author Calculations

population of the United States increased by only 11%, while the number of people in the workforce grew by an incredible 29%!

Women, too, now identified with a career outside the home and considered it a sign of success in life; especially if they managed to juggle the demands of a family as well.

Not only is the Boomers' fierce work ethic disproportionate to the wealth of the society they were raised in; it stands out from the generations before and after. The Boomers' parents were not typically driven to climb the corporate ladder. For these children of the recession, the simple financial security of having a job was often sufficient. They were paid for eight hours of work a day, and spent evenings and weekends with friends participating in family-oriented activities.

The Spock Babies
raised Super Spock Babies.

Similarly, the children of the Boomers put greater emphasis on their personal lives. Unlike their Boomer parents, they work to live, not live to work. Boomer bosses complain about a lack of work ethic in the younger generations, but it is more a matter of values. The Spock Babies have raised Super Spock Babies. They neither see their employment role as defining them, nor do they wish to emulate the single-minded focus on success they saw in their parents.

(A pause here to discuss my generational generalizations. I certainly know slacker Boomers, and many Gen Xers and Millennials who work hard. Every broad brush misses spots.)

By 1986, as the first Boomers turned 40 years old, the term "work/life balance" had entered the American vocabulary. For many people, career advancement had stepped to the forefront of priorities and family time, while perhaps not secondary, had certainly become less emphasized. Status was claimed by title and position. In vast numbers, members of the "Me Generation" unequivocally affirmed "I am what I do."

1.6 "I am what I own."

Identifying with career and position didn't do away with the need to amass copious amounts of consumer goods as badges of success. Boomers were acquisitive, and their possessions became another analog for defining success.

In the mid-1970s an interesting phenomenon arose regarding people's willingness to discuss the price of personal possessions. While their Depression-era parents had boasted to friends about great deals and opportunistic acquisitions, Boomers began to take pride in telling people how *much* everything cost.

"We found that coffee table for less than $85" morphed into "You know, we paid $850 for that coffee table." Of course, such conspicuous consumption requires justification, so the market for branded luxury products (by which a Boomer could differentiate himself or herself from friends) exploded.

Labels became the way to announce the price of goods without being so gauche as to name the actual dollar amount. Blue jeans, sneakers, purses, outerwear, wristwatches and even cars became the symbols of prosperity by which (Boomers hoped) others judged their success.

By 1985, the youngest Boomers were entering the workforce. The United States was already by far the biggest economy in the world, over three times the size of the next closest country (Japan) and larger than the next seven economies combined. The impact of the Baby Boom generation was driving the longest sustained economic expansion in history.

With a broad middle class enjoying high percentages of home and automobile ownership, automatic appliances and entertainment systems, positions and possessions became the yardsticks by which Boomers measured themselves against each other.

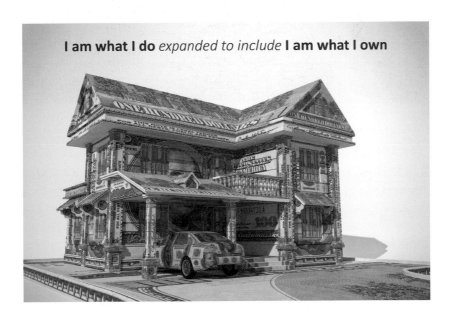

I am what I do *expanded to include* **I am what I own**

Part Two

The Small Business Boom

2.1 The Entrepreneurial Surge

To quote Jeff Goldblum's character in Jurassic Park, "Life finds a way." An influx of highly educated workers, motivated to succeed and raised with the expectation of upward mobility, won't stand on the sidelines for long.

Educated and aspirational,
Boomers overwhelmed executive-track job openings.

In 1975, the first Boomers turned 30 years old. The millions who were squeezed out of Corporate America had no intention of watching life go by without getting their due. Denied the pathway to the corporate executive suite, they chose, in vast numbers, to fend for themselves.

The United States has always been ranked at or near the top of the list of easiest places in the world to start a new business. There are no special qualifications required, and 40 years ago there were far fewer government regulations.

Moreover, small independent businesses have been a fixture of the American economy since colonial times. Even after World War II, challenging logistics (no Interstate Highway System) encouraged consumers to purchase close to home. There was no need for a "buy local" initiative to support Main Street USA.

Shut out from the corporate fast track by their sheer numbers, a maturing generation of Boomers decided that business ownership was the alternative route to the lifestyle they expected. As always, they chose that path in record numbers.

In the decades leading up to 1975, new business formations in the United States had grown incrementally from under 250,000 annually to about 300,000. Then the 30-something Boomers stepped up. Between 1975 and 1986, the formation of new businesses in America almost doubled, from 300,000 to over 500,000 annually.

1975 - 1986: 30-something Boomers more than doubled the rate of new business formations.

By 1990, when the oldest boomers turned 45, the number of new business formations had fallen back to 450,000 a year. It remains at that level today. Although the U.S. population grew from 190 million in the middle 1980s to over 320 million today, the number of business startups has remained flat. Once again the Boomer Surge created a one-time shift in a major component of the American economy. Not surprisingly, it has not been duplicated since.

U.S. Business Formations

1976:
First Boomers
Turn 30

Data Sources: U.S. Census Bureau, Chegg Study, U.S. Government Publishing Office, and Author Calculations

Most of these new businesses were "bootstrapped," or based upon the personal work of a founder with little or no capital at startup. Many of these grew to enterprises with revenues in the millions, tens of millions, and even hundreds of millions of dollars. According to the U.S. Small Business Administration, small businesses in the United States (those under 500 employees) account for almost two-thirds of all the new jobs created in this country.

How did all these new businesses find customers? Just as importantly, how could all these neophyte entrepreneurs learn the myriad of skills required to operate a small business? There were two major factors that made it feasible for these millions of new owners to find success; the outsourcing of family life and franchising.

2.2 The Outsourcing of Family Life

We've gone on at some length describing not only what drove the Boomers to seek material success but also the ways they accomplished it. Longer work hours, two income families, and a prioritization of steadily greater consumption throughout a career path combined to have one inevitable effect.

There was a lot less time for home and family.

Making the money necessary to support a competitive, upscale lifestyle takes time, and Boomers chased that upscale lifestyle in every aspect of their lives. Piling into the family car for a long drive to the lake was not nearly as fun (or as impressive to your friends) as flying to a tropical beach resort. Carefully patching a torn jacket or repairing a broken bicycle is time-consuming. It's far easier, faster and more gratifying to simply purchase a new one.

**More income and less time
created a market for disposable products.**

Successful Boomers no longer had the time for summer evenings spent leisurely teaching their sons how to play catch in the backyard. Little girls couldn't stand next to their mothers after school watching them cook a traditional evening meal. Mothers came home late and dinner now often meant assembling frozen, canned, or dried prepared ingredients. While mom was still responsible for the majority of household chores, a full working day left her with little time and energy to do anything "from scratch."

This time crunch conflicted greatly with the Baby Boomers' carefully nurtured drive to be the best at everything. Children, in many ways, had become another visible validation of success. A child's ability to perform well at their chosen pastimes, succeed academically, and lead a fully rounded life became an obsession for large numbers of Boomer parents.

Boomers invented a new sport... competitive parenting.

The Boomers had extended their aspirational instincts to a new area – competitive parenting.

The Spock Babies were raised to believe that the emotional welfare of the child was paramount. Boomers believed that emotional welfare could be greatly enhanced if their children were given the tools and opportunities to outstrip those around them.

A healthy mind in a healthy body meant children needed outdoor activities. The explosion of Little League was only the beginning.

Dad had neither the time nor (perhaps) the skills to teach the finer points of baseball, but is wasn't a problem when private coaches were available. Individual coaching led to all-star teams, premier leagues and traveling clubs. This expansion of third-party support quickly spread to organized volleyball, softball, hockey, soccer, basketball and virtually all children's sports.

As a child, I received a couple of piano lessons from a neighbor who played piano. That was pretty much the extent of my private lesson career. Our children, on the other hand, had paid instructors for martial arts, gymnastics, baseball, piano, viola, singing, and math. While that sounds like a lot, they were far from being the most coached kids I knew.

If Dad had to go to the business on Saturday morning, it was obvious that he couldn't simultaneously be washing the car and trimming the lawn. Those things got outsourced. If evenings were occupied by sports activities, there was little room for parental participation in anything besides a bit of homework.

Professional tutoring allowed one child to be dropped off for advanced math while another went to karate lessons. In between, a parent could swing by a drive-through for dinner. As a result, a lot of "family time" was being spent in the car.

Interviews with Influencers

Geoffrey "Geof" Brown

Geoffrey "Geof" Brown, CAE, is the Chief Executive Officer of the National Association of Personal Financial Advisors (www.napfa.org), the country's leading association for Fee-Only financial advisors. The organization has over 2,700 members managing in excess of $50,000,000,000.

"Our focus really isn't about the Boomers, as much as it should be about the generation that will inherit 16, 17 or 18 trillion dollars' worth of assets."

I don't foresee any shortage of practitioners in our profession. We are just now experiencing the broad emergence of undergraduate and graduate programs in the field of financial planning. Young people are starting to come out of college with planning as a specific career goal.

I think that as long as there is access to capital, the opportunities for employee or management buyouts will continue to increase. There are more opportunities for people taking over existing companies.

Our focus really isn't about the Boomers, as much as it should be about the generation that will inherit 16, 17 or 18 trillion dollars' worth of assets. They will have more flexibility, and Generation X has between 12 million and 15 million fewer bodies than the Boomers.

As a Generation Xer myself, I told my parents that I didn't want to work 60-hour weeks. Corporations are chasing younger workers with benefits and more flexibility. The days when you could say to a young employee "I want you to come in early, stay late, and work as hard as I do, or else you are a bad employee," are over.

Boomers wanted more time to generate income, and that meant focusing on efficiency at home. Time savings started in the kitchen. Kneading dough and slicing vegetables had long since stopped being the norm, but even the chores of shopping, or opening and heating food became problematic for working mothers. It was easier to take the kids someplace where they could get a hot and tasty meal at a reasonable price. "Fast Food" was the answer, and by 1975 the industry leader, McDonald's, began installing drive-through windows for those who didn't even have the time to sit down together for dinner.

As the Boomers entered each phase of life, they created huge market opportunities. By 1983, the Chrysler Corporation had figured out how to attract busy parents who spent their days running from one place to another. They introduced the minivan, an automobile chassis with car handling but also a big, boxy, seven-seat interior.

Vehicles were designed for eating,
and restaurants were redesigned for vehicles.

The minivan was designed for young families. Sliding side doors allowed easier entry for children. A rear cargo hatch prevented the kids from having to share a seat with the groceries or sports gear. One feature was by far the biggest hit – cup holders. For the first time, an automobile was designed to facilitate simultaneous eating and driving.

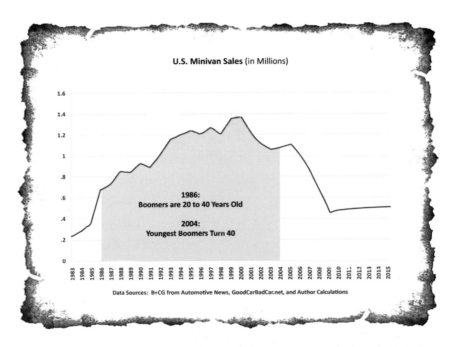

Housecleaning, home repair, gardening, and auto maintenance were all contracted out to third parties. Once again, the Boomers were focused on having it all. They could achieve work/life balance by stealing time for job and family from the mundane chores of daily life. All they needed to do was work a little harder, and make a little more money to pay for it.

2.3 The Rise of Franchising

Although many might like to think so, Baby Boomers were not born with a special entrepreneurial gene. They were simply looking for a way to survive. Despite the fact that they are 2 ½ times more likely to own a business than members of the preceding or following generations, most of those who started up in the 1970s and 1980s didn't possess a proprietary product or revolutionary method.

> Boomers weren't born
> with a special entrepreneurial gene.

Franchising came to the rescue. Franchising existed since the late 1800's, but consisted of licensing exclusive territories to make or sell a product. In the middle 1940s, three companies began offering "turn-key" businesses. Frank Wright and Roy Allen at A&W Root Beer, Howard Johnson with his eponymous motor lodges and Harlan Sanders at Kentucky Fried Chicken were the pioneers of this new business model. Franchises offered an alternative path to executive income. All they required in return was a little cash up front and a willingness to work hard for long hours.

If any generation was predisposed to work hard for long hours, it was the Baby Boomers. By the early 1980's, the average managerial work week had increased by more than 10 hours.

Franchising took off:

- Restaurants
- Landscaping
- Beauty salons
- Handyman services
- Auto mechanics
- Housekeeping
- Tutoring
- Coaching
- Dry cleaning
- Event catering ...

Franchising skyrocketed like no business proposition before it. They served food, of course, but quickly the franchise model grew to encompass mowing lawns, tutoring children, repairing cars, housekeeping, home repairs, cutting hair and doing laundry. In short, Boomers created businesses to do the things other Boomers wanted to outsource.

The shift from manufacturing in the 1980s
was driven by Boomers serving Boomers.

By the 1980s, the U.S. economy had transitioned from a dependence on manufacturing for jobs to one that was 70% generated by services. The total number of manufacturing jobs was not yet declining (the move to Asia was fifteen years later). The Boomers drove their own expanding economy by doing things for each other.

Boomers serving Boomers was the ultimate realization of their competitiveness. As small business owners, they were freed from the restrictions of Federal Wage and Hour laws. They could work as many hours as they wished!

Productivity was driven by small business owners who worked long hours cutting suburban lawns, so that they could pay a tutoring franchisee to help their children excel in their studies. The owner of the tutoring school taught as many students as possible so she could pay to have her house cleaned by a franchisee who paid another to change her oil, which in turn left him with little time for cutting his lawn.

It was an economist's dream. The velocity of money reached blinding speed. It changed hands from small business to small business, each run by someone who was motivated to produce as much as possible so that he or she could spend the resulting revenue immediately.

It doesn't take a Ph.D. in economics to understand the impact. Start with a generation that is 50% larger than its predecessor. Put about 30% more of that group (women) into the workforce. Have most of those wealth generators extend their average productive week by another 20%.

The result was the Boomer Surge, *a tripling of the U.S. economy between 1975 and 2005.* It took 200 years for America to exceed $5 trillion of Gross Domestic Product. In just 30 years, the Boomer Surge grew it to almost $15 trillion.

2.4 The Baby Bust

As we've discussed, an economy will grow if it has a steadily increasing number of new consumers and workers. If that growth curve had remained constant in the United States, the population would be some 40 to 50 million more people than it is today. In the 1980's, the adult Boomers were hitting their stride, but they weren't done changing things yet.

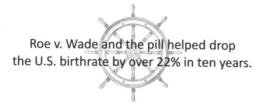

**Roe v. Wade and the pill helped drop
the U.S. birthrate by over 22% in ten years.**

The impact of legalizing birth control in 1964 wasn't gradual. The birthrate immediately plummeted from 4.0 million in 1964 to 3.5 million in 1966, a drop of over 12%. Following the Supreme Court *Roe v. Wade* decision in 1973, the birthrate fell to 3.1 million in 1975, its lowest level since World War II.

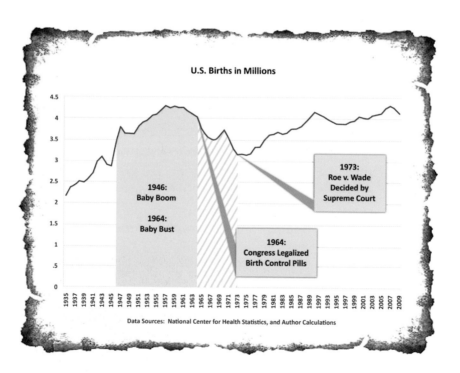

As any parent will agree, children are clearly the single greatest demand on any couple's time. The Boomers were just beginning their quest for material success, and the option of delayed childbearing gave both parents an opportunity to further their careers before being distracted by children in the family.

Generation X, commonly considered to be those born from 1965 through 1982, has nearly 30 million fewer people than the Boomers. Proportionately, the Boomers added about 56% to the population; the Xers added 25%.

Returning to Peter Drucker's quote, "I don't predict the future. I just look at what has happened already and point out the inevitable result." This has already happened. Predicting the inevitable results is merely a matter of following the numbers to their logical conclusion.

Generation X, with 30 million fewer people,
are the most likely buyers for a Boomer business.

For exiting business owners, Generation X is the group, currently 35 to 50 years old, which forms the most likely buyers for a small to mid-size business. Generation Xers differ substantially in their values, entrepreneurship, and financial capabilities than the Boomer generation they follow. The differences are impactful enough to warrant a closer examination.

"Forget the fiscal cliff, the sequestration cliff and the entitlement cliff. Those are just symptoms. What America really faces is a demographic cliff."

- The Wall Street Journal

PART THREE

The Marketplace

3.1 Your Buyers

Not every Boomer is a workaholic and I know quite a few hard charging Generation Xers. So the first thing to remember as a Boomer business owner is that Generation X buyers aren't nonexistent. There are just a lot fewer than the number of sellers because of their headcount, values, and options.

Today Baby Boomers own the majority (between 50% and 60%) of all privately held businesses that employ between 5 and 500 people. The youngest boomers, 50 years old in 2015, are already beginning to think about their retirement. The looming question is, to whom will they sell these millions of companies?

Why Not Millennials?

For the purposes of this section we are going to focus on Generation X, people born between 1965 and 1982, as the most likely buyers for an owner-operated business. Midmarket and larger companies typically have a different set of buyers, which we will address in the last section. In a small business, one with less than $5,000,000 in revenue, your buyer is likely an individual who intends to purchase a lucrative self-employment opportunity.

Many readers of my weekly column (www.awakeat2oclock.com) and attendees at my presentations ask me why I don't focus on the

Where are the buyers for the millions of Boomer Businesses?

Millennials when I discuss this topic. Since the oldest Millennials were born in 1983, they are just reaching their mid-30s today. They share some of the traits of Generation X but their overall direction is much harder to determine.

Millennials were raised in the era of social media, where individual electronic communication replaced the mass information outlets that so influenced Baby Boomers. They have differing attitudes towards the role of technology in their daily lives, and have the potential for careers that are based more on knowledge and less on hard work.

The 80 million Millennials offer bright hope for the eventual resurgence of the consumer and worker driven economy; but the impact of the Great Recession, along with educational debt, has materially delayed their career paths and family formations. It will be another ten years before they become a major factor in the acquisition of small businesses. That will be too late for at least half of the exiting Boomers. For that reason, we will stick with the Generation X buyers for our discussion.

The Perfect Storm

The tidal wave of the Boomer Surge in the economy has passed, although most business owners are only just now coming to realize it. As if things weren't dramatic enough, the multiplier synergy of the Boomer Surge is being followed by the Perfect Storm of Generation X.

The multiplier synergy
of the Boomer Surge
is being followed by
the Perfect Storm
of Generation X.

The so-called Perfect Storm occurred off the coast of Massachusetts in 1991, when three separate storm fronts came together and combined to create one of the most powerful meteorological events ever witnessed. In our scenario, three large and powerful trends are combining to form a buyers' market that is the mirror opposite of the flood of businesses seeking to be transferred.

These trends are the psychographic characteristics of Generation X, the demographic results of the birthrates of a half-century ago, and the sociographic trends of the employment environment. Like the Perfect Storm, all three combine to multiply the impact of each.

Sociographic Trends

Demographic Trends

Psychographic Trends

3.2 Psychographic Factors

Potential buyers in their 30s and 40s today differ from the Boomers in their values, life objectives, and financial habits.

Values

Gen Xers have turned Boomer attitudes regarding work/life balance upside down. While boomers say, "I am what I do," the Xers say, "What I am has *nothing* to do with what I do." Work is simply the activity that affords them the means by which to enjoy their lives. For Boomers, work and "living life" are often indistinguishable.

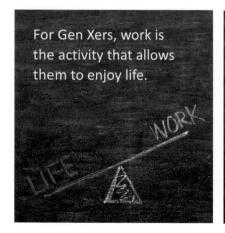
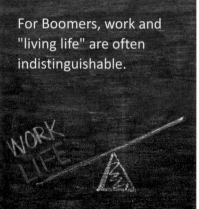

For Gen Xers, work is the activity that allows them to enjoy life.

For Boomers, work and "living life" are often indistinguishable.

What Baby Boomer business owner *hasn't* complained about the work ethic of the younger generation? Many would be well advised to remember the work ethic of their parents. Work was something that was accomplished in the span of 40 hours a week, and the rest of the time was their own.

Generation X has a work ethic
much like that of the WWII generation.

Gen X doesn't have a bad attitude towards work, they merely have the same attitude as the Boomers' parents did. Work is something that should be kept in its place, given as much time as is appropriate, and not be carried home with you at the end of the day.

Life Objectives

For Gen Xers, personal happiness is the first priority. This makes them much less likely to take interest in a brick-and-mortar business where the hours are dictated by the needs of customers. Coming to work early every day to open or staying late to close a retail establishment is contrary to this value system.

Similarly, any business that involves on-call responsibilities is considered a nonstarter. This doesn't bode well for the millions of service franchises run by Boomers. Many of those will be absorbed by multi-unit owners or become corporate stores. Many others will simply close.

Another aspect of Generation X's life objectives involves material possessions. Although many Boomers have a tough time accepting this; it's really beginning to look like Generation Xers are less inclined to accumulate all the "stuff" that Boomers take such pride in. Whether they portray themselves as Grunge, or Goth, or Eco-conscious, relatively few of their numbers are on the acquisition lifestyle track.

Relatively few Gen Xers are on the acquisition lifestyle track.

Many were raised in comfortable surroundings provided by their parents, and expect to enjoy the same lifestyle as adults. When asked how they plan to achieve it, however, a large portion point to a future inheritance. They're not far wrong, since the Boomers are the wealthiest generation in history. They are expected to transfer some $16 trillion ($16,000,000,000,000) in assets to their offspring; an amount roughly equivalent to one year of the U.S. Gross Domestic Product.

**Baby Boomers will transfer
about a year's worth of U.S. GDP to their heirs.**

(A side note: In 2015 Congress passed a sizable and "permanent" increase in the limits of inheritance exempt from taxation. Apparently, the Boomers still have substantial political influence.)

I was speaking to a business owners' group in South Carolina a few years ago. As I often do, I took a generational poll of the audience at the outset. To my surprise, about half were Generation X and Millennials. (Usually it runs about 75% or more Boomers.)

I asked these young entrepreneurs if they wanted to learn about a great business opportunity. All said that they did. I then said "All I need you to do is promise to work 50 hours a week or more for the next 20 years." They interrupted me with their laughter.

None were willing to make that commitment. I then asked the Boomer owners, "How many of you have worked over 50 hours a week for the *last* 20 years?" Almost all of them raised their hands.

Younger entrepreneurs want to own businesses. They just don't want to own *your* business if it means doing so will interfere with their personal lives.

Financial Habits

The third psychographic trait of Generation X is the financial structure of their lives in the era of easy credit.

In the 1980s, the U.S. financial industry spent millions of advertising dollars convincing people that the only smart way to enjoy a higher quality of life was to buy what you coveted now, and worry about paying for it later. The Xers have lived with debt payments since they were teens, and frequently started a permanently indebted lifestyle while in college.

Once in the workforce, Gen Xers typically spend the first part of their careers living life to the fullest and at the maximum lifestyle that their paychecks will support. Entry-level college graduates expect that a late model car, matching furniture and a substantial electronic entertainment center are prerequisites for starting independent life.

Interviews with Influencers

Kevin Mayeaux

Kevin Mayeaux, JD, CFE is the Chief Executive Officer of the National Association of Insurance and Financial Advisors (www.naifa.org), serving as the chief advocate for over 200,000 insurance agents and advisors nationwide. Kevin received his undergraduate, graduate and law degrees from the University of Florida.

"The economy will continue to grow, but as Baby Boomers remain active into their 70s and 80s, they are postponing career retirement, and even afterwards are often moving on to a second act."

Clients at every income level can expect to live into their 70s, 80s and beyond, so financial advisors must prepare to serve this large population and provide value beyond selling products and managing investments. As their lives and careers progress, Boomers will need advice on a broader range of topics. Financial advisors are frequently involved in decisions relating to lifestyle management, such as questions concerning health and wellness, and adjustments to living environments that meet the needs of an aging population.

The economy will continue to grow, but as Baby Boomers remain active into their 70s and 80s, they are postponing career retirement, and even afterwards are often moving on to a second act. At NAIFA, we have programs that help our members map out succession plans for their businesses, and to teach them how to help their clients do the same.

The future for our industry will require a lot of nimbleness. There is so much more information available to the customer today through online services and communities. Gone are the days of "kitchen table" advice, when your insurance agent would come to your house to discuss your needs. While many of our members still make house calls in their hometowns, they have to be better prepared and more informed than ever because clients have the option to do their own research prior to seeking advice. With so much information available online, consumers need professional advice now more than ever to help guide them through the multitude of offerings and determine which products and services are right for them.

"Work-Life Balance" used to mean that you worked very, very hard so that you could spend the earnings on recreation. The younger generations perceive the purpose of work as providing enough wealth to cover their needs. After that, their time is more important to them than money.

A paycheck is now widely regarded as the budget for debt payments. The concept of setting aside a substantial portion for future purchases is gone. This lack of a savings ethic jibes poorly with the amount of equity many Boomers have built in their companies. Those businesses cannot be acquired without substantial capital investment; an investment most Gen Xers simply don't have, and in reality can't imagine.

If cash flow doesn't support outside financing,
you will be the lender of last resort.

Sellers can assume that a large percentage of Gen X buyers will expect easy payment terms for their acquisitions. If the cash flow doesn't support third-party financing, a seller will, by default, become the lender of last resort.

3.3 Demographic Factors

Americans spend almost $200,000,000 a day on lottery tickets. They know that the odds against winning a jackpot are astronomical. The average person could spend his lifetime earnings on tickets and not substantially increase the likelihood of winning.

Owners who plan to sell to Gen Xers with a bucket of capital and a desire to work 60 hour weeks are similar. Someone like that is out there, but would you stake your life's work on the odds?

Size Matters

No one can change the birthrates from 1946 through 1964 any more than they can change those from 1965 through 1982. The first date range produced 78 million people, the second 48 million. When we overlay the spike in birthrates from the 1950s and early 1960s with the trough of the late 1960s and 1970s it provides a startling comparison.

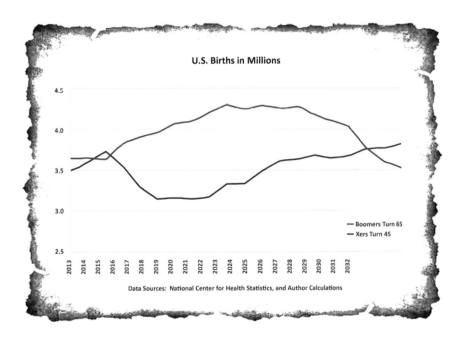

U.S. Births in Millions

Data Sources: National Center for Health Statistics, and Author Calculations

Beginning in 2018, the number of Baby Boomers reaching 65 years old will exceed the number of Generation Xers reaching 45 years old by just over 2,000 people daily. Two thousand people a day equals 60,000 people a month, or about 750,000 people annually, for the next 10 years.

If we assume the need for a one-to-one relationship between sellers and buyers, the statistics would be dramatic enough. Considering only 3% of the population of each generation are typically business owners, the shortage between the Boomer sellers and Gen X buyers would be 60 owners a day, or over 20,000 annually.

Statistically, over 50,000 businesses a year may not find a buyer.

But the Boomers are more than twice as likely to own a business, and the Xers less likely to. The number of businesses for whom selling to a next-gen owner is statistically unlikely, may be as many as 50,000 a year.

I'm not trying to inflate this realization for dramatic impact. The calculation for Boomer owners is, if anything, conservative. That's just how the numbers work out.

A Great Sucking Sound

In his presidential campaign of 1990, H. Ross Perot famously characterized the economy as suffering from a "great sucking sound" emanated by the industries taking jobs from the United States to Mexico.

The first half of the 21st century will be dominated by a great sucking sound, but it won't be from foreign competition. It will be generated by the massive costs of providing entitlement programs to the Baby Boomer generation, just as they withdraw their disproportionate productivity from the workforce. Retirement of the Boomers currently accounts for about half of the shrinkage in the American workforce.

> *"My fellow Democrats will have to accept that no amount of new taxes can make up for changing demographics"*
>
> - Senator Erskine Bowles, co-chair of President Obama's Committee on Tax Reform

Some economists predict that the lost production of the Boomers will be made up by new technologies. Machine learning and robotics experts are predicting that computers will soon be capable of replacing up to 40% of today's jobs. That may be so, but we're still a long way from leading the leisurely existence of HG Wells' Eloi (in *The Time Machine*) while C-3POs produce enough wealth to pay for everything.

> *"Politicians must now confront the difficult trade-offs they avoided during years of steady growth and easy credit. Many democracies now face a fight between past and future, between inherited entitlements and future investment."*
>
> - The Economist

In the 1970s and 80s, at the height of the Boomer workforce surge, there were five active workers paying into the Social Security system for every retiree. Today there are four, and in ten years there will be three.

The other half of the workforce shrinkage is due to a lack of new workers coming into the economy. The Baby Boom and Bust are eroding the employment base from both ends.

Not only will far fewer Boomers be paying employment taxes, many of their assets are sheltered. Tax-advantaged retirement plans and capital gains on home sales are the two largest sources of retirement funding for Baby Boomers, and neither pays into Social Security.

This exact problem has plagued Japan for two decades. In two more, the shifting demographics of the historical one-child policy in China will explode to crisis levels. The Southern European nations are experiencing it now.

The ratio of workers to retirees
is falling to an all-time low.

It's difficult to say how much pressure this will put on the U.S. economy, but thinking that it will be substantial doesn't require prognostication. For small business owners, it will likely translate into stagnant markets, recurring recessions, or deflation.

Supply and Demand

This is the most obvious demographic effect, so we don't have to take a lot of time with it.

**Prices fall when
there are more sellers than buyers.**

We're all familiar with the theory of price elasticity. What happens to business values when there are more sellers than buyers? They go down, of course.

As we noted earlier, for hundreds of thousands of businesses coming to market over the next twenty years, there will simply be no buyers. It's difficult to overstate the disparity in numbers. We aren't merely talking about discriminating buyers, or reluctant buyers, or less qualified buyers. There are simply not enough bodies for the number of businesses that will be available.

This is the driving force that multiplies the third generational storm: the Sociographic wave.

3.4 Sociographic Factors

Gen X thinks and acts differently from Boomers. Just as importantly, society, especially business society, treats them differently.

The Benefits Battle

The average Main Street employer has never been on level ground with large corporations when it comes to offering competitive lifestyle benefits. Just as plainly, smaller employers are often more reluctant than big business to reduce their workforce as a first step in cost savings.

Attracting and retaining workers from Generation X and the Millennials will require that small businesses leverage an area of clear advantage; they know all of their employees personally. This allows them to offer individual or "customized" flexibility that isn't available in larger organizations.

As long ago as 2008, the ability to find workers to replace retiring Baby Boomers was ranked as the *number one* concern among CEOs of large international corporations. Their organizations employ economists and futurists who are able to tell them how dramatic the coming storm will be.

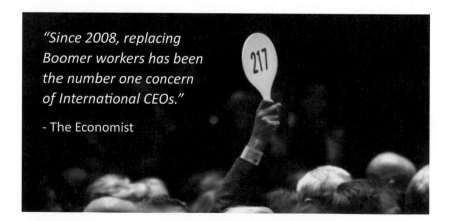

"Since 2008, replacing Boomer workers has been the number one concern of International CEOs."

- The Economist

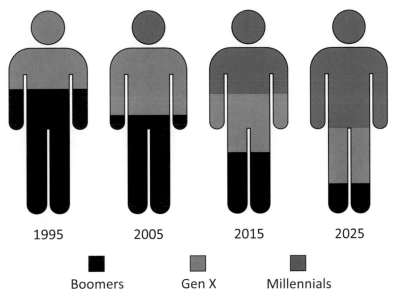

U.S. Labor Force by Generation
(Silent generation (1925-1944) not shown)

| 1995 | 2005 | 2015 | 2025 |

Boomers   Gen X   Millennials

Source: US Bureau of Labor Statistics, and Author Calculations

Unfortunately small business owners are far less aware of the problem, and are in many ways unable to address it. They can neither afford the workplace benefits to compete with those offered by corporations, nor are they inclined to treat the next generation of workers differently from their own generation.

Small business owners
have to compete with corporate benefits.

As we've discussed, Generation X has very different values and life objectives than their predecessors. Corporate America understands that completely, and has moved aggressively to accommodate them. Few small businesses can match the flexibility introduced in the corporate workplace in the last fifteen years.

Flexible hours:

Employees arrive early to leave early, or arrive late and stay late, or take time during the week and work on weekends to accommodate their family activities. The lockstep march into the office at 9:00 AM and the mass exodus at 5:00 PM are things of the past. Employees are more frequently judged on their results, and in most large businesses, taking time off for personal tasks or errands no longer raises an eyebrow.

Telecommuting:

Technology has not only made working from home possible, it is saving corporations millions of dollars when they provide less workspace, parking, mass transportation reimbursement, and cafeteria lunches. While the socialization aspects of face-to-face groups is still critical, many companies allow half or more of their employees to work remotely on any given day.

Paid time off:

Maternity leave, paternity leave, family medical leave, time off to care for aging parents, sick children, and a wide variety of paid, partially paid, and unpaid time off without penalty has spread far beyond traditional "sick days."

Job sharing:

Companies are increasingly willing to work with several part-time employees or even independent contractors in positions where it is difficult to find a full-time wage earner.

Portable benefits:

The ability to transfer and keep your benefits when changing from one job to another is increasing. This eliminates another barrier to changing employers.

Paid external interests:

Sabbaticals, paid continuing education, paid assignment to community service organizations, and a host of other programs are promoted by the large companies seeking to attract Generation X and the Millennials.

Almost every business has implemented some of these "modern" benefits, but smaller companies usually need their employees on-site to deliver their products and services on a day-to-day basis. They don't have sufficient redundancy in any position to comfortably sustain long periods of time off for a key person.

Boomer owners still expect employees to arrange their personal lives around the demands of the workplace. These attitudes, considered so elementary for Boomers, are often looked upon as onerous and uncaring by next generation workers.

Many business owners say that it isn't Generation X that they have problems with in the workplace as much as the Millennials. As the aging Boomers remain active workers later in life, they are more exposed to colleagues and employees who are four and even five decades younger than they are.

Exacerbating this is the relative lack of Generation Xers in the workplace. Many small businesses grew and maintained their business primarily by employing Boomers in all but the most entry-level positions. As the Boomers begin to age out of the workplace, those companies are finding that there aren't enough Generation X candidates to take their place.

By 2020, the Millennials -- people born from 1982 onwards, will account for over 50% of all employees in the workplace. Unfortunately for business owners, they will still be a decade or more from becoming viable acquirers.

3.5 The Law-driven Society

In the 1970s, the legislative atmosphere in the United States began to shift. Prior to that time, justice was an area that was more dependent on the judiciary than lawmakers.

"There ought to be a law" became the watchword. Busy Boomers turned to their elected representatives to solve issues that seemed to be exploding out of control.

In the 1950s and 1960s, judges frequently dealt with delinquency by telling young men to join the military to avoid a conviction record that would haunt them for the rest of their lives. With the explosion of street drugs in the 1970s, crime and criminals rapidly grew beyond the capability of a local judge to administer slaps on the wrist.

Not only did the resulting laws regulating sentencing quickly fill up our jails (the United States has the largest percentage of incarcerated citizens in the world), but the attitude that laws could be made to control all sorts of behavior became commonly accepted.

Federal agencies, using constitutional authorization to regulate interstate commerce as a springboard, stepped into every aspect of business life. OSHA's oversight of workplace safety quickly extended to the use of extension cords and the height of stair risers.

The Environmental Protection Agency expanded from controlling toxins to dictating the disposal of virtually all workplace waste.

The Consumer Protection Agency, started to prevent fraud by crooked businesses, was soon dictating the exact language of loan agreements and home-improvement contracts.

The Food and Drug Administration expanded its mandate to oversee the purity of ingredients; going so far as to encompass the appropriate temperature of a cup of coffee. The Department of Labor, formed to make sure people were paid according to the Federal Wage and Hours Act (1938), grew its mandate through ERISA and EEOC to regulate all benefits, both tangible and intangible, offered to any employee.

In 2015, the Federal Government published 81,611 pages of new and proposed rules, an all-time high.

This expansion of employer liability and regulatory oversight has made it a lot tougher to go into business for yourself than it used to be. It's a small wonder that many of the presumed buyer generation show little interest in taking on the responsibilities of being an employer.

3.6 Disintermediation

As we've discussed, Boomers in the 1970s and 1980s created a substantial shift in the U.S. economy by focusing less on manufacturing and more on services. With future generations of business owners less inclined to embrace brick and mortar concepts, it might seem that service companies would be easier to sell.

That may not be the case. It isn't strictly a generational issue, but it is important enough to address in any discussion about selling Boomer businesses.

"Of course your job is secure, Bob. I don't know
how we would get along without you."

Disintermediation is the elimination of intermediaries between consumers and producers. Technology has been replacing lower-tier jobs for some time, but the reach of the Internet is expanding into the middle strata of professionals and well paid non-professional positions as well.

New businesses launch daily based on disintermediation, with models that eliminate the people and their traditional "value added" services from the middle of a transaction.

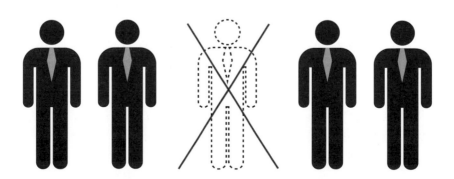

Interviews with Influencers

Paul Viren

Paul Viren, CLU, ChFC, AEP® is the President of Viren and Associates in Spokane, Washington. He also serves as the President of the National Association of Estate Planners and Councils (www.naepc.org), a professional organization of 29,000 individual members active in estate planning for clients. He holds that organization's Accredited Estate Planner® certification.

"I observe a 'mirage effect' among Baby Boomers. Their exit is always two more years down the road."

I see a resurgence of entrepreneurism in the United States as Millennials get their chance. They are optimistic, and have greater access to financing. There is a real chance for them to shine if the regulatory environment doesn't stifle them.

Generational transition is a challenge for our profession, however. The average age of my clients is about 55 years old. Younger people don't put the same value on face-to-face contact and building relationships. Online accounts and robo-advisors encourage them to navigate their financial world without personal relationships. We have to stay on top of current technology, but that also leads to fee compression, and lowers our ability to look ahead at what the client's needs might be in the future.

Many financial planning firms are handed down to family members. In the Association, we are focusing on communications between generations, because the transfer process can be awkward and clumsy if it isn't planned and implemented well.

I observe a "mirage effect" among Baby Boomers. Their exit is always two more years down the road. They are taking on the financial burdens of parents and children, and often of their grandchildren. Those outside responsibilities erode their personal security, and delay the ability to retire.

When it comes to business transfers, I'm seeing more ESOPs (Employee Stock Ownership Plans) than I've seen in a long time. Younger owners are seeking a lifestyle from the business, and aren't enthusiastic about the sacrifices required by the traditional Boomer entrepreneurial workload that accompanies solo ownership.

The "gig economy"
disconnects employment from earning a living.

These disruptors enable the "gig economy," allowing individuals who value their independence to choose when, where and how they work. They offer their services directly without the constraints of a traditional job with a typical company. A few hours a week spent on graphic design or reading X-rays online, supplemented by a couple of nights driving for Uber or Lyft, can satisfy many peoples' financial needs.

The same technology promises to cut swathes through the service industries. Here are some examples, not from a science fiction book, but rather easily tracked in the daily newspaper (which represents yet another threatened industry).

Self-driving trucks can move freight during low-traffic periods, and don't need food or rest breaks along the way.

If you use credit cards for most of your purchases, your bookkeeping program can already prepare a standard tax return with minimal input from you.

Corporate audit standards can be met using programs that will choose accounts for confirmation, generate communications and track their receipt.

*Case law for courtroom briefs can be assembled using
voice search of legal databases.*

*Robo-advisors will manage your retirement portfolio,
responding to changes in market conditions with lightning speed.*

*Real Estate for Sale by Owner (FSBO)
consolidators bypass high agent commissions.*

*Computer Aided Design (CAD) programs can allocate building space,
add switches and outlets according to code, and generate Bills of
Materials for transmission to wholesalers or manufacturers to quote.*

*Online insurance brokers sell health care, auto and
liability coverage for all but the most complex cases.*

*Lending sites price loans competitively using your ubiquitous
credit history, and are moving into business finance.*

What does this portend for the future of the banking, insurance brokerage, architectural, real estate, finance, legal, accounting, and transportation industries?

A successful service company generally follows a standard business model. It sells knowledge, usually the ability to navigate an important but complex process, or sometimes (as in trucking) the ability to consolidate individually uneconomical activities like moving products to specific destinations.

A successful service company first sells value,
then purchases the service for less.

The service company then "purchases" its capabilities for less than their selling price. In most cases, that means hiring skilled people who execute the tasks required. For many small professional practices, hiring a handful of such people produces enough margin to support a "business." The skills of marketing, selling, and handling the most difficult situations rests with the owner.

However, without those producers, or when they are contracted in remote locations and paid by the "gig," it becomes a real question of whether there is actually a company at all. It's difficult to see why a buyer would pay any premium to sit alone at a computer.

As a result, the owners of such companies, particularly those with twenty or fewer employees, may not have a saleable business model. Apart from their customer list, there is little in the way of intrinsic assets supplementing the work of an individual owner. As disintermediation continues to spread through the service sector, it becomes one more reason why Boomer-built service businesses will struggle to transition.

3.7 Entitlements

Many Boomers are quick to criticize the debt driven lifestyles of Generation X and the Millennials. They are, however, quick to ignore their own generation's role in running up the biggest unfunded liabilities in history; Social Security and Medicare.

The unfunded liabilities for Medicare exceed the entire market value of the mortgage derivatives behind the Great Recession.

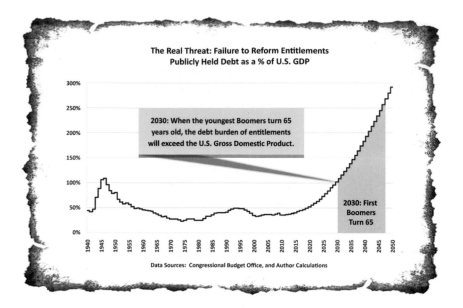

The Real Threat: Failure to Reform Entitlements
Publicly Held Debt as a % of U.S. GDP

2030: When the youngest Boomers turn 65 years old, the debt burden of entitlements will exceed the U.S. Gross Domestic Product.

2030: First Boomers Turn 65

Data Sources: Congressional Budget Office, and Author Calculations

To be fair, neither Social Security (founded 1935) nor Medicare (1966) were the products of Baby Boomer voters and legislators. For well over a half-century, the benefits were paid out to the generations prior to the Boomers, those who had actually contributed little to the system. Supporting these financial burdens was easy as long as the largest, hardest working generation in history was footing the bill.

Now the bill for the largest group of retirees in history is coming due. Although eligibility for collecting full benefits from Social Security has been raised slightly from 65 to 67 years old, it clearly hasn't kept pace with the realities of life expectancy.

"There simply is a limit to the extent to which we can save today in exchange for leisure and high consumption tomorrow. Somebody has to do the work tomorrow; we cannot all be retired by that time."

- Richard Baldwin, Graduate Institute of Geneva

When Social Security began, the average American could expect to live 67 years. Today a male's life expectancy is over 76 years, and a female's is slightly over 81 years. In the same timeframe the ratio of working adults to retirees has dropped from 5:1 to 4:1. It will be closer to 2:1 when all the Boomers retire.

Medicare liability is even more dramatic. The total estimated cost of caring for the Baby Boomers is approaching $60 trillion. For a comparison, that is roughly the amount of all the outstanding mortgage derivatives that almost sunk the U.S. economy in 2008. Most of the derivative money was never paid, but Boomers certainly expect that their healthcare bills will be.

The entitlement burden on the up-and-coming generations is a problem that our political system has been completely loathe to address. There are a limited number of solutions. But one of them or a combination of several has to be chosen.

> By the time all of the Boomers retire,
> there will be two workers for every person collecting benefits.

The Boomers may see their benefits dramatically cut. Stiff new taxes could be levied on the following generation. The United States as a nation may simply decide to amass a breathtaking debt at the expense of all other government programs, and hope the Millennials will pay it off. Regardless of the approach, it's guaranteed that a very large number of people will be extremely unhappy.

Some sociologists predict a war between the generations. While that will hopefully be avoided, it is certain that the next generation's ability to chase executive-level compensation by bootstrapping a small privately held business will be severely curtailed.

3.8 The Generation X Business Buyer

The combination of the three trends, and the compounding effect each has on the others, bodes poorly for the sellers of brick and mortar businesses. The aspiring Generation X acquirer is entering a buyers' market, driven by the laws of supply and demand. He or she doesn't have much money to buy a business, and has been raised to expect that easy financing terms will be built into any major purchase. He doesn't want to work long hours, be tied down to a specific location, or be required to curtail family activities.

Even if the Gen Xer is entrepreneurially inclined, he is facing an escalating risk of going into business for himself, without the fair wind of a 40-year economic expansion.

Let's put everything in one place for the full impact.

There are far fewer buyers than sellers.

Those buyers are less inclined to make the sacrifices many small businesses demand, and have little capital for acquisitions.

They are also being actively pursued by the larger companies that formerly had no room for the Boomers, and which have the resources to offer more lucrative, secure and flexible working environments.

Gen X buyers are fewer, poorer,
and less attracted by Boomer lifestyles.

The businesses being sold are overabundant, operating in an increasingly difficult regulatory environment, and are likely to face demographically driven stagnation in the economy.

Compare this to a statement made to me by more than a few Baby Boomer business sellers. "This business will provide me with a nice retirement. When I get tired of it, I'll sell it to some young person just like me who is willing to work really hard and pay for a great opportunity."

Some people are lucky; but for most that's a pretty poor plan.

Part Four

Winning Starts with a Plan

Part Four: Winning Starts with a Plan

I've supplied enough information for you to understand why planning for your exit now is better than waiting. The dynamics of the coming buyer's market will be challenging, to say the least. Like any competition, the race will go to those who are best prepared.

Like any competition, the race will go to those who are best prepared.

Let me make something plain. I'm not a doom and gloom kind of guy. I've built successful companies with little or no capital, poor resources and lots of hard work. If I worried about the odds, I never would have gone into business for myself.

You can beat the Boomer Bust, but you aren't likely to do it armed with only luck. The rising economic tide of the 40-year Boomer Surge is over.

> *"In the 4th quarter of 2012, for the first time, Baby Boomer retirement was the number one reason driving business sales."*
>
> - Pepperdine University/IBBA/M&A Source Market Pulse Survey

To be blunt, you're like the hiker running from the hungry bear. You don't have to be faster than the bear, you just need to be faster than the other hikers.

Advance planning can dramatically increase
the post-tax proceeds you receive from your business.

Today, Boomers in their late 60s are starting to sell the businesses they've built over the last 30 years or so. They represent just the tip of the iceberg. Millions more are steadily approaching their career finish lines at a rate of hundreds daily.

4.1 What the Heck *is* Exit Planning?

Yet again, Boomers as a consumer group are attracting attention. Exit Planning is a new discipline, developed to meet a massive market need. Unfortunately, like any new service offering, there are a lot of people who use the term without fully understanding it, or in hopes that it will associate them with a growing field of professional practice.

Accountants say they do Exit Planning when they help clients structure their business and personal holdings to minimize the bite of the IRS.

Estate attorneys say they do Exit Planning when they protect assets and document transfers of inheritances.

Wealth managers say they do Exit Planning when they provide retirement projections and validate lifestyle assumptions.

Consultants say they do Exit Planning when they recommend ways to increase the value of the business, presumably maximizing the proceeds from a sale.

Business brokers say they do Exit Planning when they value and list a company for acquisition.

Insurance brokers say they do Exit Planning when they write policies to protect owners, their families and their companies against premature departures, or the absence of key employees.

Which of these professionals *really* do Exit Planning?

There are two answers: 1) All of them 2) None of them

Exit Planning is the process of developing a strategy for
the biggest financial transaction of a lifetime.

Exit Planning is the process of developing a business owner's strategy for what may be the biggest financial transaction of his or her life...the transfer of the business. That strategy may be a succession to the next generation of family. It could be a sale to employees. It may be a sale to another entrepreneur, competitor or acquisition by a larger company. In some cases, it might require an orderly dissolution.

Exit Strategies

| Succession | Sale to Employees | Sale to another Entrepreneur | Sale to a Competitor | Acquisition | Dissolution |

In every case, it involves tax, legal, financial, operational and risk management expertise. No one practitioner has all the knowledge required for every aspect of the plan. Exit Planning, in the true sense of the word, is coordinating all those skills so that they work together for a single objective.

Exit Planners coordinate their skills
and work together toward a single objective.

Some owners try to coordinate the various professions in the belief that he (the owner) knows what will work best for him. That approach doesn't work in any other business situation.

Let's say, for example, you run a warehouse with delivery services. You decide to make it as efficient as possible.

☞ *You tell the purchasing manager to only order product when pricing and inbound freight are least expensive.*

☞ *You tell the warehouse manager to develop a system for picking orders with methods that require the least amount of labor.*

☞ *You tell the shipping department to pack up orders using the least possible amount of material.*

☞ *You tell the dispatcher to plan routes for times with the least traffic and the lowest fuel use.*

☞ *You tell the sales department to promise the customer anything that will close the sale.*

Now, without letting any of these people talk to each other, you announce that you are implementing all of their results simultaneously. That night you dream about how profitable your business is about to become.

You don't have to be a distribution expert to know what is going to happen. The uncoordinated plans are going to explode when combined. Backorders rise, because the purchasing manager waited until cost-effective qualities could be shipped. Deliveries are outside of customer-convenient hours. The parts aren't coordinated. You've just come up with a great way to go out of business.

Now, what if you told one manager that your overall goal was to sell more product and give excellent service, so customers would become loyal buyers and the company would increase revenues and profits? Then you had the other managers report to him, so that all of their plans would complement the overall objective.

That's what an exit planner does.

"It looks like another owner needs his goals defended."

An exit planner is the defender of the owner's objectives. He or she coordinates the efforts of other professionals so that they complement each other. In the course of developing and implementing a plan, different advisors will inevitably have differing approaches. One may prefer a certain legal structure that creates specific tax benefits. Another might be more knowledgeable about income sheltering approaches that require a different legal model.

Professionals from various disciplines
may have differing approaches to planning an exit.

An exit planning professional is knowledgeable enough in multiple disciplines to weigh different approaches and discuss them with the business owner. He or she is also a coach, keeping the discussion of technical approaches within the framework of the client's personal vision.

Coordinating various disciplines at the outset
can generate substantial savings on professional fees.

There are few consultants who only offer exit plans. Most came to the specialty through another avenue, so your planner might be an accountant, attorney, financial planner, or another business advisor. Whomever you select to lead the process, it should be someone that you trust to act in your best interest.

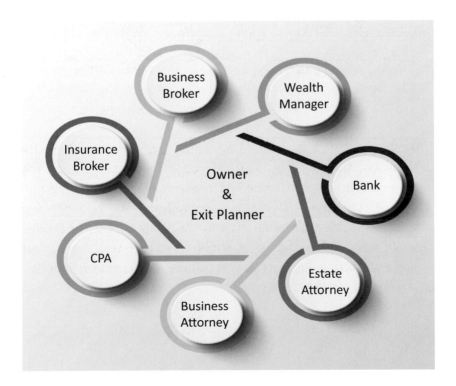

Tales from the Trenches

Nancy and Frank Kudla

A member of the first class of female cadets to graduate from the United States Air Force Academy, Nancy built dNovus RDI from a one-person consulting company to over 350 employees, recognized by the SBA as National Small Business Contractor of the Year.

As befits Nancy's strategic training, she and her husband (and CFO) Frank began planning their exit five years in advance, retaining the most prominent investment banking firm in their industry. They carefully identified the fundamental value of their business, focusing on core strengths and trimming areas that didn't add to its worth.

When they took dNovus RDI to market, their intermediary presented the package to over 50 likely suitors, and began accepting initial offers. But even the best plans can run into surprises.

The Best Laid Plans...

We were excited about the number of businesses who expressed interest. Then the financial markets collapsed in October, 2008 and everyone disappeared. It made no sense to me, since for most of the prospective buyers the cost of dNovus RDI would be a miniscule part of their multi-billion dollar operations. None the less, almost all of the buyers ran for the hills.

The funny thing was that the most attractive buyer remaining wasn't even in our industry. They weren't on our initial top ten list, or quite honestly on our top fifty. They wanted an entry point to our markets very badly, however, and were willing to go forward when all the others balked. And just as significant to us, they loved our company culture and seemed to recognize its importance to our success.

The final price ($38 million) wasn't everything we hoped for, but it was more than what we personally had set as our trigger point. Just as important, they accepted one of my key conditions – that Frank and I walk away on the day of sale, and not spend one day working for someone else.

On the first day following the closing, Frank and I kept checking the bank balance on our phones to make sure it was true. It's not a bad outcome for someone who never considered herself an entrepreneur, but more stumbled into it and found out that I was pretty good.

The money is great, but I spent most of the first few years afterwards dealing with serious medical issues. I believe they were related to the years of ignoring my own health while building the company. I've always been driven, but now I try to remember the advice of a high school teacher. "Remember to stop and smell the roses." And they do indeed smell sweet!

4.2 The Last Competition

Boomers are the most competitive generation in history. Their behavioral profile developed in a strange world of scarcity (due to their numbers) in a time of plenty (also due to their numbers).

Don't make the mistake of thinking
that the Boomer competition is over.

The mistake many business owners are making is thinking that the competition is over. There is still one more race to run.

Like the Pig in a Python, a sharp statistical increase represented as a bulge in an otherwise level pattern, Boomers created markets, drove economic development, and changed societal mores as they hit each of the stages of life with hurricane force. What goes up must come down, and the massive creation of small businesses in the 1970s and 1980s will inevitably, not maybe, *but inevitably*, lead to a massive sale of businesses between today and 2030.

Like the Pig in a Python effect, Boomers created markets, drove economic development, and changed societal mores as they hit each of the stages of life.

Now you can better understand the reason for the rapid expansion and use of the term "exit planning" in the last few years. Ten thousand Boomers turn 65 every day, and as with every previous Boomer surge, an industry is developing to cater to their needs.

10,000 Boomers
turn 65 every day, and
another industry
is developing to cater
to their needs.

Preparing to cash out of your business, which is likely the largest single financial event of your career, is going to be more difficult than it would have been even ten years ago. The days when you could telephone a business broker, list your business, and within a few months find another Boomer to buy it, are coming to an end.

Business Brokers will sell
less than one in ten Boomer companies.

This isn't new. It's just the latest incarnation of Boomer competition. Like every phase before it, some people will have great success, many will do enough to come out okay at the end, and some will, by default, finish at the end of the line.

4.3 The Basics of Planning

There are certain things you have to know in order to begin planning a rational and successful exit from your business. These aren't optional, and we strongly advise that you put some effort into making sure your baseline information is accurate. Everything else in your plan will be developed from these basic building blocks.

Triangulation

Every exit plan starts by plotting three points of critical information. The first represents where you are now. The second indicates where you need to go. The third shows how much time you're willing to take to get there.

| Where you are now | Where you need to be | Preferred timeframe |

Where you are now is usually a pretty straightforward calculation. It is your present liquid net worth. This may include a stock portfolio, income property and other assets. We recommend calculating your net worth *without* your business, for reasons we will discuss in a moment. We plot your current worth as the left point in a triangle.

Every journey requires a starting point,
a direction and an ending point.

If you haven't had a retirement financial plan done using inflation and life expectancy assumptions, you should do it now. Many of our clients are surprised to find out that they have already saved enough to retire comfortably. About an equal number are shocked to discover that they will run out of money long before they run out of years.

In most cases, we work with a Certified Financial Planner (CFP) or a CPA with the Personal Financial Specialist (PFS) designation for these projections. Some insurance agents or non-CFP financial planners also have software that is suitable for providing an analysis.

A comprehensive financial plan requires considerable review of your various investments and assets. It includes not only your retirement savings, but insurance policies and debt commitments such as mortgages. Most planners expect a separate fee for doing a complete analysis, although some will do it without charge if you are already a client or they hope that you will become one.

I have one word of warning. If a planner is doing projections based only on your completion of a questionnaire, without examining the underlying documents and assets, it's unlikely to be a top tier plan.

This planning, which we term a Financial Needs Analysis, allows you to set the right end-point of the graph. This represents your ultimate financial goal.

The next step is to choose your exit date. This may be defined by two deadlines, one for when you step back from operating the business on a day-to-day basis, and another for when you leave the company permanently. Committing to an actual end date is critical to any reasonable planning. It is easy to say "I'll retire when I have $3 million," but it makes a big difference if you need to have that amount in the next year or the next decade. Your exit date is represented at the apex of the triangle.

Here is an example of a simple triangulation.

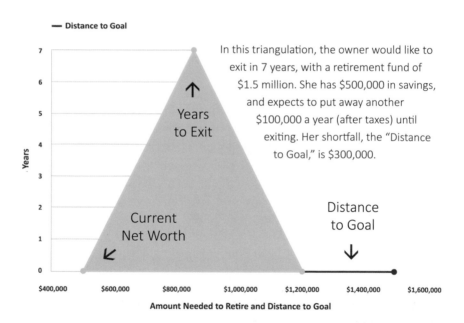

In this triangulation, the owner would like to exit in 7 years, with a retirement fund of $1.5 million. She has $500,000 in savings, and expects to put away another $100,000 a year (after taxes) until exiting. Her shortfall, the "Distance to Goal," is $300,000.

Note that the triangle shows your current net worth as the left-hand base point, and your future need as the right-hand terminus of the graph. The base of the triangle from left to right is your ability to save towards your target in your chosen time frame.

The difference between the right base point of the triangle and your target is the "Distance to Goal." This is the amount after taxes that you must realize in order to fully fund your financial objective.

Once you have triangulated the broad parameters of your exit strategy, you can begin planning scenarios. For many owners, reaching the goal might require a longer timeframe than originally anticipated, and the triangle will get taller. For others, the timeframe is the most important criteria, so they choose a retirement lifestyle that may be somewhat less luxurious than what they originally anticipated.

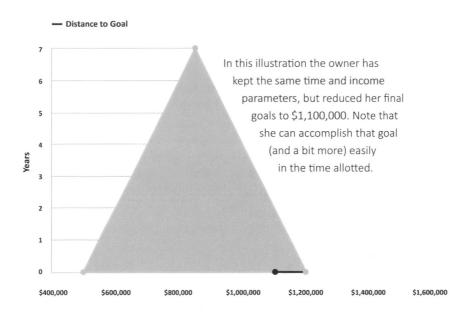

In this illustration the owner has kept the same time and income parameters, but reduced her final goals to $1,100,000. Note that she can accomplish that goal (and a bit more) easily in the time allotted.

Test your strategy by graphing triangles with real metrics. For each year of "height," use an equal distance across the base to measure one year of available retirement cash contributions (savings-years) from your business. You now have a quick graph of your plan's practicality. Changing different factors may have a surprising impact.

You can triangulate your own scenarios with the free tool at **www.YourExitMap.com**.

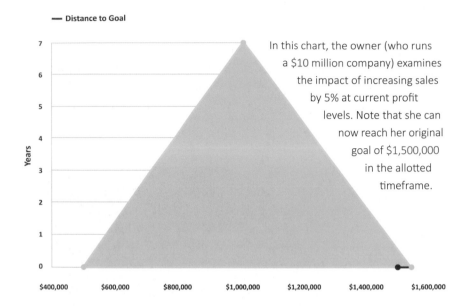

— **Distance to Goal**

In this chart, the owner (who runs a $10 million company) examines the impact of increasing sales by 5% at current profit levels. Note that she can now reach her original goal of $1,500,000 in the allotted timeframe.

Triangulating your financial exit plan serves several ends. First, it acts as a reality check. It also allows you to test the impact of increasing profits, extending your time frame, or adjusting your final goal.

Once you've settled on a plan you like, it creates the basis for your future business planning.

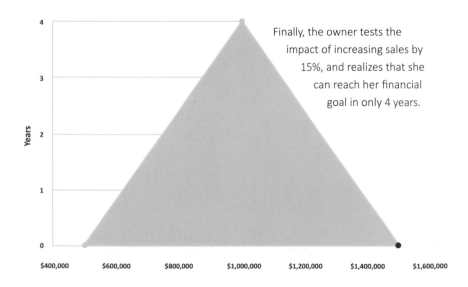

Finally, the owner tests the impact of increasing sales by 15%, and realizes that she can reach her financial goal in only 4 years.

Valuation

Valuation is one of the least understood aspects of an owner's business. Anyone who tells you what the value of your business is by using sentences that begin with, "All small businesses are," or "Companies in your industry sell for," or "I know someone who sold a company just like yours," is likely to be giving you bad information.

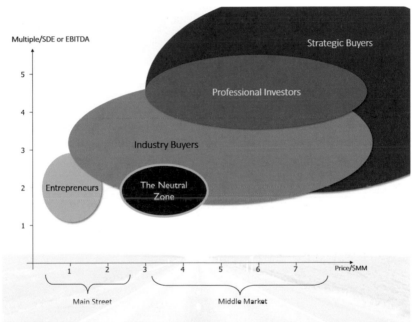

Watch the 2 minute video on buyers and valuations at **www.yourexitmap.com.**

I cringe when I think of how many times I've heard business owners say something like, "I know what my business is worth, because I talked to a guy at a trade show who knew somebody in another state who sold a business that I think was about my size and a lot like mine, and he said he got five times revenue... or was that five times earnings... or maybe it was five times cash flow."

Few owners pick a number out of thin air and then base their entire life plan on it. The problem is, many test their theoretical number on

Many owners confirm their concept of value
with "financial experts."

several "financial experts" whom they believe confirm it, and then move forward, treating it as a reality. Here's how that happens:

A business owner applies for a business loan. Of course she is asked for her personal financial statement. For practical underwriting purposes, the bank will lend the money based upon the cash flow of the business; its ability to repay the loan. Nonetheless, the lender wants the owner to personally guarantee repayment, backed by her personal net worth.

When the owner calculates her personal net worth she puts the business down with a value she thinks is in the ballpark. The banker accepts it without question, because it has little to do with whether the loan is approved or not. In the business owner's mind, financial "expert" number one, the bank, has just signed off on her valuation.

"With a business this successful, you'll have no trouble retiring in comfort."

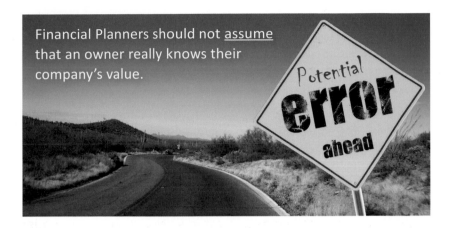

Financial Planners should not <u>assume</u> that an owner really knows their company's value.

The owner next visits a financial planner to calculate her potential retirement lifestyle. Again, she presents her personal financial statement with an estimated value for her business. The planner uses it to begin developing her retirement scenario.

I've given a number of presentations about valuation to financial planners. I'll ask "How many of you do retirement planning for business owners?" Usually most of the attendees raise their hands. My next question is "How many have business owner clients who list 70% or more of their net worth as the value of their business?" Most of the hands remain raised.

Rumor, hearsay and newspaper articles
are not valid methods of valuation.

My next question is "Who here insists on a third-party valuation of the business before they develop a retirement plan?" Surprisingly, most of the hands go down.

It's puzzling to me how a plan can be built around an owner's subjective opinion for 70% of its assumptions, but I understand the problem. Most planners assume that an owner knows what the business is worth. After all, it is the client's industry and her livelihood. Certainly she would have accurate information about her biggest asset.

In the case of our business owner, this is how the second financial expert, her planner, has confirmed the company's value. In reality, the owner's opinion of value may be based on hearsay, faulty statistics or projected wish fulfillment. In fact, I've seen owners submit a number that is anywhere between half and ten times what the real Fair Market Value of their business is.

In a few cases, they've planned around this fantasy for years in the belief that someone would have told them if there was a problem with it.

Business valuation is an area where I strongly recommend hiring a skilled professional. While I've seen a substantial number of accountants who claim to be able to do business valuations, I would never utilize one that didn't maintain an Accredited in Business Valuation (ABV) or Certified Valuation Analyst (CVA) credential in addition to his or her CPA. Other certifications that

utilize the Uniform Standards of Professional Appraisal Practice (USPAP) include:

- Accredited Senior Appraiser (ASA): American Society of Appraisers

- Chartered Financial Analyst (CFA): CFA Institute

- Certified Business Appraiser (CBA): Institute of Business Appraisers

Business brokers or business marketing services will frequently offer a free opinion of value as part of their listing services. Some have free online tools where you can calculate a business' value for yourself. While an experienced broker can be pretty accurate in his estimate of sale price, there is ample reason to take the extra step of getting an appraisal by a paid, certified professional.

A broker has vested interest in offering a value you will accept. I've known brokers who will accept any value the owner wishes, in the belief that the marketplace will eventually bring the client to reality. In other cases, an aggressive broker may set a value that favors a quick commission.

In a third party sale, a broker's opinion is fine as long as you understand that buyers, and their advisors, will give it no credence at all. For an internal sale (such as an ESOP or LOB), or for estate planning purposes, you should understand that this type of valuation will not be accepted by the Internal Revenue Service or lenders.

Once you have a concrete, objective evaluation of your business you will be better prepared to determine the improvements needed to cover your Distance to Goal. It will also help you test the practicality of your timeframe.

Tales from the Trenches

Bill and Jeanne Pippin

Bill bought Stanbio Laboratories as an unwanted division of his European employer, using an SBA loan for the purchase. Over the next two decades, he built it into a leader in reference laboratory diagnostic reagents and proprietary medical diagnostic equipment. He moved the company from an old industrial site to a beautiful suburban campus of his own design.

Bill was approached by EKF Diagnostics, a global supplier in the same market space. Although he wasn't actively seeking an acquirer, Bill knew that a well-matched strategic buyer offered an ideal opportunity. He sold Stanbio in a cash transaction, with no earn-out or contingency other than a two year employment agreement with incentives.

When a Child Leaves Home

After I sold the company, things really didn't feel much different. It was fun to check my bank account, but the owners were far away, and I continued working with the same employees. It really came home, however, when I wanted to do something I thought was best for the business and was countermanded by the new owner's upper management.

The due diligence was lengthy and exhausting. I was ready to call the whole thing off more than once, but I had great attorneys who kept things on track. They also did a wonderful job of protecting me against many of the post-closing price adjustments sought by the buyers.

I had such an emotional attachment to the business. We built a park-like campus. There is a stream flowing past the front door, and a later addition has a glass wall that looks out on a waterfall. I worked on the design personally, and hand-picked every piece of furniture and all the fixtures.

More importantly, I had always felt responsibility for the employees and their extended families. So many people were depending on me to make the right call. Selling the business was like having a child leave home, but surrendering that burden, just knowing that someone else made the ultimate decisions, was a relief.

Today I am an angel investor and serve on several advisory boards. I purchased another small company, but the customers and personnel weren't a cultural fit for me, so I sold it. My wife Jeanne and I are focused on traveling, dividing our time between our three homes and the grandchildren. We're very conscious of how lucky we are to be able to do these things while we are still young enough to fully enjoy them.

Multiples of What?

When discussing the selling price of a business, most offers are discussed in terms of multiples. Depending on the type of business, its size, and the buyer, multiples may be used to mean price calculated in terms of revenue, profit, or cash flow. There isn't any hard-and-fast methodology.

Valuation uses cash flow, assets and comparative business sales to determine approximate value. In order to really comprehend your possible proceeds from a sale, however, you need to clearly define your value in terms of multiples.

Understanding the value of your business requires an understanding of *what* is being multiplied when price is discussed. Revenue, profits and cash flow are terms that both owners and professionals use when discussing valuation multiples. They not only mean different things, but the same term may mean different things in different scenarios, or even to different people in the same class of buyers.

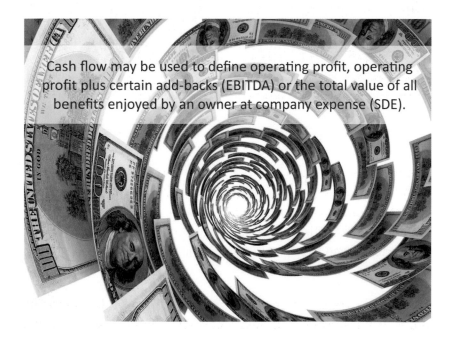

Cash flow may be used to define operating profit, operating profit plus certain add-backs (EBITDA) or the total value of all benefits enjoyed by an owner at company expense (SDE).

Multiples of revenue aren't commonly used as a standard measure of value, but it does occur. Some technology businesses, especially creators of proprietary software, are frequently sold for multiples of gross revenues. Such multiples may also be used to describe the price of professional practices, even though the real price is actually being determined by profitability.

For example, accounting firms and insurance brokerages are commonly discussed using a rule of thumb of 1 to 1½ times revenues as a price guideline. This isn't necessarily because revenue is truly the measuring stick. It's just an easy way to refer to pricing in industries where profitability is fairly predictable across a wide range of companies.

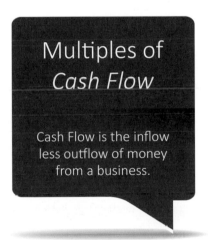

Multiples of
Cash Flow

Cash Flow is the inflow less outflow of money from a business.

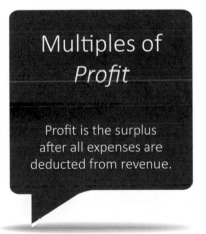

Multiples of
Profit

Profit is the surplus after all expenses are deducted from revenue.

The majority of industries discuss value in terms of multiples of cash flow or multiples of profit. These terms are frequently used interchangeably, although their meaning is different. "Cash flow" is a particularly difficult term to nail down or define since different segments of the merger and acquisition (M&A) world use it to define various calculations.

"Profit" is more concrete and customarily the term for operating profit from normal business activities before taxes. On the typical corporate tax return, that would be line 21 from which you calculate your tax liability. Although some people use profit to mean operating profit plus certain add-backs, that is more correctly a definition of cash flow.

"Cash Flow" can mean any number of things. The most restrictive usage is the Statement of Cash Flows prepared as part of financial reporting. It shows the sources of cash during the period and its uses. It is a good management tool, but has very little to do with valuation.

The most expansive definition of cash flow is frequently used by business brokers in Main Street (under $3 million) listings. These are businesses in which the buyer is usually an individual seeking to purchase a job. He or she intends to work full-time in the business, and make a living from it.

Those businesses are valued by Seller's Discretionary Earnings, or SDE. SDE is calculated by combining the pretax profits with the owner's current salary, and then adding back all the other benefits he or she enjoys from the business. These might include an automobile, health insurance, life insurance, vacations (recorded as business trips), the casual employment of children, and other personal expenses.

Some owners add back the casual employment of children.

Many small business owners live, to some extent, out of the business checking account. They might be writing off gas for the family car or using a company Netflix account at home. These are clearly economic benefits that accrue to the owner, and are appropriately included as part of the value of the business. (An SDE calculator is available for free at www.YourExitMap.com.)

"Main Street" valuations
usually include owner benefits.

Of course valuations vary widely. I have already warned you about the hazards of considering a "typical" valuation of any business, but a decent rule of thumb is that the majority of Main Street businesses sell for between two and three times SDE.

Formal, professional valuations are limited
by USPAP standards and IRS-approved methodologies.

Like most such numbers, these are grounded in practical realities. If an individual buyer plans to put 20% down and finance 80% of the purchase through a third-party lender, three times SDE is about the limit at which he or she can expect to acquire the business, receive a return on the down payment investment commensurate with the risk, draw a salary, and maintain a reasonable debt service ratio for the lender.

You can calculate your own Seller's Discretionary Earnings using the free SDE Calculator at **www.YourExitMap.com**.

Seller's Discretionary Earnings (SDE) Calculator©

DISCLAIMER: This worksheet was developed to help and owner analyze the full value of ownership. We make no representation regarding the tax deductibility or legitimacy of the expenses listed. Many of the items contained herein might be regarded adversely by a lending institution, and some (such as unrecorded cash) are downright illegal. Consult your professional advisor before making any representations based on this worksheet.

Fiscal Year Ending (Date): 12/31/2017	Seller	Notes
Gross Sales:	$4,358,912	
Less Cost of Goods Sold	$1,875,364	
Gross Profit:	$2,483,548	
Less G&A Expenses	$1,998,852	
Pre-Tax Profit:	$484,696	
Owner's Salary and Benefits:		
Salary (per IRS return)	$150,000	
Bonuses	$42,500	
Distributions		
Est. Payroll Taxes on Owner	$23,100	
Owner's Insurance (Annual Premiums):		
Life Insurance	$8,456	
Health Insurance	$9,685	
Other (non-auto) Insurance		
Owner's Vehicle(s) to be Retained by Owner:		**Note:** To be considered discretionary, a vehicle must not have a primary business use. A delivery truck that is taken home at night, for example, shouldn't be included.
Annual Finance Payments:	$11,258	
Insurance	$3,574	
Fuel	$1,596	
Maintenance and Repairs	$2,544	
Non-Producing Employees (Family):		
Salary		
Taxes		
Retirement		
Personal Expenses		
Education		
Vehicles Not Used in Business (Family):		
Annual Finance Payments:		
Insurance		
Gas		
Repairs		
Insurance (Family or Other):		
Life		
Health		
Other		

Spouse Salary Adjustment:		Note: Spouses (or other family members who work in the business) may have wages above or below the market rate for a similar position which could impact SDE.
Spouse's Position	Bookkeeper	
Current Annual Salary	$75,000	
Market Salary (see note)	$45,000	
Difference	$30,000	

Owner's Personal Expenses (Non-Business):	
Entertainment	$5,000
Travel	$11,500
Legal	
Accounting	$2,500

Residential Expenses:	
House Payment	
Landscaping	
Utilities	
Telephone	$355
Janitorial	
Repairs	$2,566
General Discretionary Expenses	
Other	

Owner As Landlord:		Note: Complete this section only if you own the business location through a separate entity.
Current Annual Rent Paid	$144,000	
Market Rent	$120,000	
Over or Under Payment of Rent	$24,000	

Miscellaneous:	
Cost of Other Assets Purchased Through Business	
Charitable Contributions	
Personal Dues and Subscriptions	$300
Merchandise for Personal Use	
Personal Legal & Accounting	
Bank Charges (Not Credit Card Fees)	$785
One Time Major Expense	
Amortization	
Depreciation	$16,587
Section 179 Expense (Excess Over Depreciation)	
Interest Expense	$45,588
Other	

Loss or Profit on Sale of Assets:	

Total Add-Backs to Earnings:	$876,590

(Less) Deductions from Cash Flow:	
Accrued Employee Salaries	
Interest Income	
Miscellaneous	

Total Deductions from Earnings:	$0

Seller's Discretionary Earnings (SDE):	$876,590.00

How realistic is the value you set on your company? Use this tool to create a sale scenario. Enter the price, expected down payment, financing and SDE cash flow. It will calculate the debt service, return on investment for the buyer's down payment, minimum buyer salary, and any free cash flow remaining for the new owner. A field whose value turns RED means that your scenario doesn't meet typical purchaser or lender standards.

Seller's Valuation Sanity Check©

Fill in values in white fields ONLY. Dark blue fields are calculated automatically.				
		Amount	**Pct.**	* Required Fields
Purchase Price		$2,500,000	100%	*
Downpayment		$600,000	24%	*
Seller Financed		$250,000	10%	*
Annual Rate	6.00%	* If Seller Financing is not used, enter		
Term (years)	5	* $0 above, and 1% for 1 year to left.		
Bank Financed		$1,650,000	66%	
Annual Rate	5.50%	* If Bank Financing is not used, enter		
Term (years)	10	* $0 above, and 1% for 1 year to left.		
Other Financed		$0	0%	
Annual Rate	1.00%	* If Other Financing is not used, enter		
Term (years)	1	* $0 above, and 1% for 1 year to left.		
Total Purchase		**$2,500,000**	**100%**	Value Must Equal 100%

Current SDE		$565,000	[1]	*
Annual Payments to Seller		($59,349)		
Annual Payments to Bank		($218,902)	Debt Coverage	149%
Annual Payments to Other		$0		
Owner/Mgr. Compensation		$150,000	[2]	
Free Cash Flow		$136,749	[3]	
			Downpayment ROI	23%

1) Seller's Discretionary Earnings (SDE) includes pre-tax profit, owner salary and benefits. 2) Owner compensation needs vary, but most lenders set a floor of about $100,000 annually for businesses valued at less than $500,000, and $150,000 annually for those worth more. 3) Most banks require free cash flow of not less than 125% of debt service. Free Cash Flow is the amount available annually for working capital, investment, and owner compensation after debt service.

In a small business, the company's cash flow will be the biggest factor in determining value. For an individual buyer, the cash flow must be enough to service the acquisition financing, pay the new owner reasonable compensation, and provide a risk-appropriate return on investment for the down payment (usually 25% or more).

The Seller's Valuation Sanity Check© tool is available at **www.YourExitMap.com**.

Companies larger than Main Street businesses are almost always discussed in terms of EBITDA. (Earnings Before Interest, Taxes, Depreciation and Amortization). This is a cash flow measure that takes into consideration an elective financing expense (interest), and two non-cash expenses (depreciation and amortization) that are deducted as tax accounting entries from the pretax profits. That cash is commonly considered available to support debt service in the value calculation.

Note that the EBITDA measurements do *not* consider the owners wages and benefits as part of cash flow. This is frequently confusing for midmarket companies that sell for between $3 and $10 million. Owners of these companies often enjoy substantial perks from the company, such as vacation homes or boats for entertaining clients. They obviously would like to include SDE-type expenses in calculating EBITDA, but the more professional buyers in that bracket are seldom interested in paying multiples of those benefits.

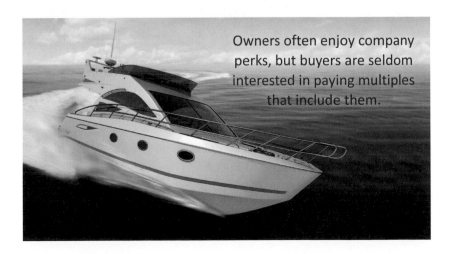

Owners often enjoy company perks, but buyers are seldom interested in paying multiples that include them.

Tales from the Trenches

Bob and Nancy Davison

BVA Scientific, a distributor of laboratory supplies and equipment, started in Bob and Nancy's bedroom, with the garage serving as the "warehouse." Both had a background in laboratory supply sales, and they focused on building deeper customer relationships than the multi-billion dollar vendors who dominate the industry.

That approach helped the company grow with a balanced customer base. BVA has a presence in food testing laboratories, water and wastewater plants and the Texas oil fields, rather than the typical dominance of doctors and hospitals in this type of business.

Not surprisingly, BVA had attracted multiple inquiries from private equity groups. None of those came with management, however, and all wanted the Davisons to remain as employees for a long time after the acquisition. While they weren't in a rush to get out the door, Bob and Nancy wanted a clear path to retirement.

"First, let's kill all the lawyers..."

Nancy: We knew that the business had grown beyond what a couple of salespeople could handle well. Supply sources were moving to Asia, and I felt a bit out of step. I think the real impetus was when a general manager to whom we planned to sell the business left for, of all things, his own sign shop franchise. We hired a replacement, but we could see that he wasn't our exit plan.

Bob: I've always been very active in our trade association. A colleague with a much larger operation had asked me several times to let him know if we would consider selling. When he repeated the offer at a conference, we decided to start talking seriously.

Nancy: The due diligence almost killed me. The buyer's attorneys kept asking for more information. Halfway through the deal their lead attorney went on maternity leave, and her replacement wanted to restart the whole process from the beginning!

Bob: Our legal bills wound up being so much more than we anticipated. I think my biggest surprise was finding out how many adjectives could be used to modify the word "lawyers."

Nancy: The closing date was delayed multiple times. Then our biggest customer told us privately that they were planning to shift their purchasing for high-volume items to China. It was a gut check, but we shared the information with the buyer. We had to restructure the deal with a portion tied to an earn-out, based on the level of business we maintained for a year after closing.

Bob: Nancy stepped back pretty quickly. I wasn't quite ready to retire, and now I have the added motivation of watching our earn-out. My role is technically sales-related, but it is just as much about keeping the employees happy through the change.

These differing approaches are buyer and market dependent. They have little to do with standard valuation formulae. In fact, they are not among the USPAP accepted methodologies for appraisal. Nonetheless, they are almost universally used in the Business Brokerage and Merger/Acquisition (M&A) industries.

Add-Backs

This confusion leads to a lot of bad advice. I often hear advisors tell clients who are planning to sell to restrict all their tax-advantaged benefits for several years in advance, in order to raise the company's reportable income. That could be beneficial, but it mostly depends on who your buyer is. If it is a Main Street level entrepreneur, it will make no difference. You will be adding those benefits into the SDE.

Some owners try to put every expense possible into SDE. They add back their cell phones ("I give out the number to customers."), dry cleaning bills ("I have to dress well for work.") and soda for the company refrigerator ("I don't have to supply that if I didn't want to.") After all, they reason that every dollar of added SDE is two, three or four dollars onto their price.

A buyer who sees endless
nickel and dime add-backs will likely be more cautious.

Keep in mind that a buyer who sees endless nickel and dime add-backs will likely be more cautious. Providing documentation that you are doing too much "under the radar," is begging for a tougher and more detailed due diligence process.

Another error made by midmarket ($3 to $50 million in value) companies is to try including SDE-style add-backs when presenting to a professional buyer. These buyers historically pay higher multiples, but are more restrictive in the add-backs they will accept.

Every owner wants to believe in the highest possible value for his or her company. Frequently this results in a "calculation" that combines the add-backs of a Main Street business with the multiples paid in the midmarket. This can create some excitement with the resulting number, but that excitement will just increase the level of disappointment when the actual offers turn out to be much lower. Understanding the proper valuation approach is much easier if you know the type of buyer that your company is likely to attract.

You can find other tools such as the EBITDA Calculator and Customer Concentration Analysis at **www.YourExitMap.com**.

Different valuation methodologies can often produce similar results.

Different valuation approaches don't necessarily lead to widely different values. In many cases, a valuation of 2.5 x SDE and one of 4 x EBITDA may be nearly the same.

The best way to get a realistic value for your business is to hire a competent business appraiser. This can and should cost money. Depending upon the type of appraisal and the credentials of the person conducting it, it might be anywhere from $5,000 to $25,000 or more.

4.4 Classes of Buyers

Buyers for privately held companies fall into certain distinct groups. There are entrepreneurial or individual buyers, industry buyers, financial buyers and strategic buyers.

Entrepreneurial	Industry	Financial	Strategic
$3 million or less. Multiples typically settle between 2 and 3 times SDE.	Small businesses in local markets usually anywhere from 2.5 to 4 times EBITDA.	Most mid-market transactions range between 4.5 and 5.5 times EBITDA.	Size plus intent to integrate and grow, could be 5, 10, or 15 times EBITDA.

Entrepreneurial

We have already discussed the individual buyer, one who is seeking a business priced at $3 million or less for the purpose of earning a living. Their range of multiples typically settle between 2 and 3 times SDE.

Individuals (occasionally partners), are usually purchasing their first business. They are unfamiliar with the process, and will often lean on their attorney for advice. Unless they are experienced business owners, their chief obstacle to executing a deal is the fear that they might be making a mistake.

Industry Buyers

Somewhere between the individuals and the professional financial buyers are your competitors, customers and vendors.

Competitors can be excellent buyers, but these transactions can be challenging for several reasons. First, the seller needs to be very cautious in sharing information during the initial negotiations. There is a danger in exposing trade secrets, customer data, or employee information that would benefit the buyer whether he completes the deal or not.

Additionally, it is difficult to ascertain the real value to a competitor when the buyer already possesses some or all of the talent and infrastructure needed to run your business. Competitors are typically not enthusiastic about paying for their potential economies of scale, but it is clearly a factor in their buying decision. There is no "standard" range of multiples for competitive sales, but for small businesses in local markets anywhere from 2.5 to 4 times EBITDA would be a realistic starting point.

Vendors and customers
may vertically integrate by acquisition.

Lumped in with competitors with regards to price range are vendors and customers. They will buy a company to secure a distribution channel (vendors) or to guarantee supply (customers.) Like competitors, they will realize some additional economies with integration, and this may raise the value of the business to them.

Financial Buyers

Further up the food chain are financial buyers, the private equity groups and family offices.

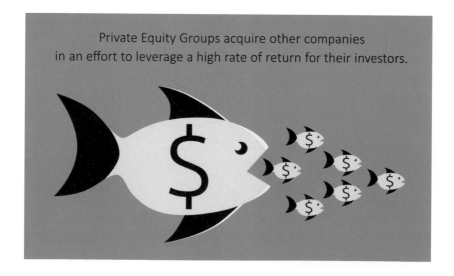

Private Equity Groups acquire other companies
in an effort to leverage a high rate of return for their investors.

Private equity groups are financial partnerships assembled for the purpose of acquiring companies. They range from search funds, where investment is promised if the right deal comes along, to large acquisition funds with hundreds of millions of dollars in ready cash. Private equity groups may specialize in an industry, or be agnostic as to the type of business as long as it produces acceptable returns.

Family offices are increasingly acting like closely-held Private Equity Groups.

Family business offices are professional investment and financial management companies that specialize in managing the wealth of one or a few high net worth family groups. Traditionally, these organizations acquire in industries adjacent to their core holdings. More recently, some have begun acting more like closely held private equity groups.

Financial buyers conduct exhaustive due diligence to protect their investors. Because of the expense of hiring professionals to dig into every nook and cranny of the company, they will seldom consider a deal when the target has less than $1,000,000 in EBITDA.

Financial buyers conduct exhaustive due diligence to protect investors.

These buyers, not surprisingly, price businesses in a fairly narrow range. This makes sense when you understand that they have investors to whom they promised a certain return. While the multiples paid increase with the size of business being acquired, for most mid-market transactions the range lies somewhere between 4.5 and 5.5 times EBITDA.

Strategic Buyers

Strategic buyers are the Holy Grail of private business sales.

Finally, we have the Holy Grail of private business buyers; the strategic acquirer. This is a very large company, possibly publicly traded, that is seeking to buy a privately held business because it provides a certain distinct competitive advantage. That advantage may be a proprietary product, service model, geographic territory, or contractual relationships.

The strategic acquirer's intent is to purchase a business and grow it exponentially by integrating it with their existing customer base. For that reason, along with their size, they may be willing to pay multiples of 5, 10, or even 15 times EBITDA.

Remember, however, that attracting a strategic acquirer requires that you have true differentiation. If they can re-create your product or market on their own, it is often less expensive to do so than pay a high multiple for your business.

4.5 The Neutral Zone

You might be reading the descriptions of the buyer classes above and asking yourself, "Where do I fit in?"

Hundreds of thousands of Boomer businesses, founded on a shoestring 40 years ago, have grown to be substantial businesses that employ hundreds of people. They provide the owner with personal income in the top 1% of Americans (over $450,000). Their companies are typically between $5 million and $15 million in gross revenue, although some may be smaller or larger than that range.

Many of these owners are stuck in what we call the Neutral Zone. They are too big to be small, and too small to be big. Their profitability prices them outside the capability of most individual buyers, but they are below the critical $1,000,000 cash flow threshold that attracts M&A (financial and strategic) industry professionals.

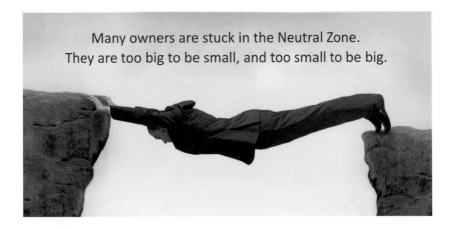

Many owners are stuck in the Neutral Zone.
They are too big to be small, and too small to be big.

Selling to employees is becoming increasingly attractive.

Thousands of these owners are choosing a growingly popular exit strategy, a sale to their employees. It's an approach that allows the seller greater control over pricing, timing, and the legacy of his or her business.

Companies in this size range usually have a fairly well-developed management team, and sufficient cash flow to sustain reasonable debt service. With proper structuring an owner can realize full Fair Market Value, choose the time of his or her departure, and remain in control of the business until receiving 100% of the proceeds.

We'll discuss sales to employees farther on in this book, but in a market where well-financed entrepreneurial buyers may be few and far between, and the effort of growing to the next level isn't appealing to the owner, it is an increasingly attractive alternative.

PART FIVE

Beating the Boomer Bust

5.1 Understanding the Odds

The bad news for Baby Boomer business owners is that they are entering a fiercely competitive market for selling small and midmarket businesses. There is some good news, however. Boomers are competitive and ambitious. They have, after all, competed at every stage of their lives. This is just a new race where once again, some will meet with enviable success, while some won't.

"How Do You Know?"

I'm often asked where I got my numbers. It isn't easy to get a solid handle on exactly how large this shift may be. My calculations came from combining pieces of data from the Small Business Administration (SBA), the United States Census Bureau and the Department of Labor (DOL) Statistics.

I expected that these organizations would have paid a little more attention to an issue this massive, but perhaps I shouldn't be surprised that it receives so little attention. After all, these are the same people who remove someone from the unemployment rolls for working even one hour in the previous month, simply because they don't want to upset the electorate with bad news.

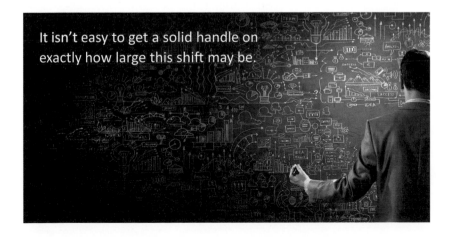

It isn't easy to get a solid handle on exactly how large this shift may be.

> Politicians know that discussing tough
> issues won't get you elected.

Our political system isn't in the business of delivering bad news. I just finished Ron Chernow's *Hamilton*, where he discusses how the first few U.S. Presidential administrations settled on a policy of always communicating an optimistic viewpoint. Politicians realized 200 years ago that focusing on tough issues won't get you elected.

Here's what I know, and what I've extrapolated.

According to the Small Business Administration, there are between 28,000,000 and 29,000,000 private businesses in the U.S. at any given time. Around 19,000,000 have either 0 or 1 employee (home based, real estate partnerships, corporate shells).

That leaves at least 9 million businesses with employees. That much we know for sure. Other sources give the same result.

From there, it gets a little fuzzier. Various studies (sponsored by grants from the SBA, DOL, or Census Bureau) put the number of businesses with five or more employees at between 6 and 9 million, and those owned by Boomer-aged folks between 51% and 61% of those. As a long-time coach to privately held businesses, I can attest that both my coaching client base of business owners and those of my colleagues around the country easily reach that percentage of Boomers.

Now we have a spread from as few as 3 million to as many as 5.4 million companies, depending on whose numbers you use as factors. I use 3 million because it is the lowest likely number. It could be much higher, but we will work with the more conservative scenario of 3 million. Now for the extrapolation.

About 3% of Americans own businesses, but from 1976 to 1985, the Boomers formed businesses at a rate almost 250% greater than previously; a percentage of the population that hasn't been approached since. The total percentage of Boomers who own businesses still appears to be more than double the average, although we don't know how many of those companies have five or more employees.

"How Many Businesses Will be Sold?"

Let's be very cautious, and say only 4% of Boomers own businesses with employees, or only a third more than the national average. Again, that is reasonably conservative.

Boomers are currently reaching age 65 at a rate of about 10,000 a day, or 3,500,000 a year. That means that at the low end (our 4% estimate), some 140,000 business owners a year are retiring or at least *reaching* retirement age (because we know that Boomer owners tend to hang on longer).

The brokerage industry currently sells about 8,000 companies a year. The mid-market (M&A and Private Equity Groups) account for another 1,000. These numbers are from the intermediary industry's own statistics.

Statistics indicate that sellers will fail to find buyers at a rate of 350 a day.

So, if we take our conservative estimate of Boomer ownership and reduce it by the full number of brokered sales each year, we are still short of buyers by about 11,000 a month, or 350 a day (including

weekends) for the next two decades. Assuming that Boomers own a higher percentage of businesses just makes those numbers worse.

That seems ridiculous. How could over 350 businesses a day disappear and not be noticed, or fail to create headlines nationwide? There are several possible answers.

First, over 6,500 people die in the U.S. every day, yet we only infrequently experience the passing of someone we know personally. Our network of friends and family is far broader than our business "network." How many times have you seen an empty storefront next to one you were entering, and were unable to even remember what business used to be there?

**Over 90% of Boomer employers
have yet to transfer.**

Understand that these numbers only project businesses that won't find a third-party acquirer. No one tracks the businesses that sell their customer list to a competitor, are bought by employees, passed on to family, or close voluntarily. Those are growingly popular options, and are completely untracked statistically.

Businesses close for many reasons. In fact, normal attrition, according to the SBA, is over 5,000 a day or 2,000,000 a year. If 350 are Boomer-owned employers; that is less than 6% of all closings.

So the lack of buyers is only important to someone who is planning on selling his or her company. Our 350 a day doesn't sound like much, but remember we aren't discussing *all* businesses, just those that support employees and their families.

These numbers are startling. If you've ever studied statistics, we are probably seeing only the third deviation to the left of the bell curve. The businesses selling in the third-party market now are largely owned by the Boomers born between 1945 and 1950, formed businesses around 1975-1980, and are turning 65-70 this year. The historical birth rates and business formation rates both indicate that the main event, about 97% of employer transfers, is yet to come.

"When Will the Crisis Hit?"

The numbers indicate that the crisis will hit between 2017, when the differential between Boomer and Generation X birthrates spikes, and 2025, when the youngest Boomers reach their 60s.

It could actually be sooner or even later than that. It could be a media driven topic of the moment, or it might pass without mention, since the majority of folks who don't own businesses have little interest in the issue.

As I said previously, some pundits believe that we will replace thousands of small businesses with technology. Think of Amazon as your store next door. Larger companies will absorb much of the available space. A high profile example is McDonald's expanding into gas stations and Walmarts, replacing local lunch counters and those in the five and dime stores.

> *In 2008 85% of business owners said they plan to sell their businesses to a third party in the next 5 years. That was 85% of 60-year-old owners, 85% of 65-year-old owners, and 85% of 70-year-old owners.* -Price Waterhouse Coopers

Many Mom and Pop stores will close quietly, because their owners no longer want them and their families no longer need them. Corner groceries in New York City passed from immigrant Italians, to Eastern European Jews, to Koreans and then to Arabs as each generation grew up, educated their children, and joined the suburban middle class.

The surge of sales may not ever be obvious. Some businesses will be sold privately without an intermediary. Many are log-jammed by owners who haven't figured out their exit yet. A substantial number of Boomers may work until age 70 or later. The youngest Boomers are still in their early 50s. They still have a while, but inevitably they will get there.

No matter what the reasons for delaying any individual exit, the fact remains: Sooner or later every owner leaves his or her business, and the transition of the Boomers will be like nothing ever seen in the business history.

5.2 Eyes on the Prize

The triangulation process described in the previous section is an absolute prerequisite before setting out a roadmap for action. Since the transfer of your company is likely to be the largest single financial transaction of your life, you really want to pay attention to the underlying drivers.

Putting a practical, well-grounded plan in place can be the difference between adding years of struggle to achieve your goals, and executing on time with minimum diversions.

Triangulation starts with knowing where you stand today. Taking inventory of your net worth and potential future income, including insurance and retirement payments, is the bottom left-hand base point of your planning triangle.

Be absolutely ruthless in your estimates of value. You may be driving a $100,000 automobile, but unless you intend to sell it, invest the proceeds in your retirement account, and drive something far less expensive, it should not be an asset for your future planning.

01	02	03
What is your net worth today?	Retirement year? How much money do you need?	Is the time frame feasable?

Similarly, the equity in your home is only going to support you if you sell it and move somewhere more affordable.

The next point to identify in your triangulation exercise is determining the right-hand terminus of the graph; your eventual financial goal. This is the amount you will need in order to retire, or progress to your next career with sufficient funds. You may not need professional help to calculate your current net worth, however, it's advisable to get some assistance with other calculations.

You can triangulate your own scenarios with the free tool at **www.YourExitMap.com**.

Tales from the Trenches

Dennis and Anna Stahl

Dennis and Anna purchased Lone Star Pet Supply from Dennis' uncle, and in the following three decades grew the local distributor over 50-fold. The company dominated the distribution of pet food and supplies market in Texas, consistently ranking in the top 10% of profitability for the industry.

Dennis and his President, Danny Selman, were tireless in their quest for greater efficiencies. As Dennis said frequently, "If you aren't adding to our margin, you're adding to our expenses."

The company was known for its leadership in effective distribution, and as an early player in Internet fulfillment for web-based retailers.

For several years, two private equity groups had been rolling up pet supply distribution. One had started on the East Coast, the other in the Pacific Northwest. Both needed a presence in Texas and southern states to claim national distribution.

At Light Speed

Of course, we were approached about selling at every gathering of the industry, but I really didn't have much interest. Between the two of us, Anna has always been more of the visionary. One afternoon near the end of a long summer stay at our Island home, she announced that we should have a "two bottle of wine dinner tonight." That was our signal that it was time for a serious talk.

That night she asked me "How much is enough?" We were very comfortable already. Danny was ready to lead the company without me, and Anna was spending most of her time at our home on the coast. We knew that we could choose our buyer, and that we'd get a solid premium over market valuations for the industry.

After consultation with Danny, I called the potential acquirer who we were most comfortable with, and told them "You are our choice. Meet our needs, and we are ready." They visited in early September, and after a three hour discussion, they asked to borrow a conference room to prepare an offer. One hour later, they returned to put a written offer on the table that took my breath away. We announced the deal in October and closed by mid-November.

I still sit on the parent company's Board of Directors, and used my relationships to help close a number of add-on acquisitions. I've done well handling the move from an eight figure to a nine figure company, but I don't know if a ten figure business is still in my comfort zone.

Anna and I sold our home near the business a few years ago. Other than being the real estate landlord, I don't go there much now. I had served in leadership positions for our church and a large non-profit before the sale. That turned out to be great preparation for both my Board role and my new job as a City Councilman on South Padre Island.

Consider having an expert calculate your retirement needs based upon estimated returns on investment, inflation, and life expectancy. You might be surprised at the amount you really need in order to support your lifestyle. I have worked with a number of business owners who were shocked to find out that what they thought was a substantial nest egg was unlikely to last beyond their late 70s.

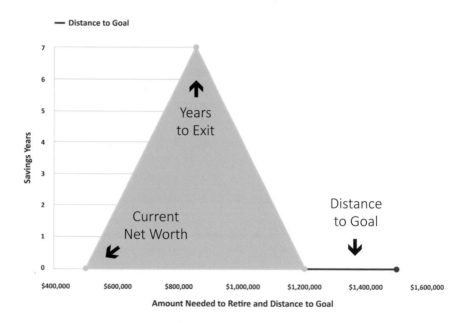

The height of the triangle, or apex, represents your departure date.

Now calculate the amount you can save from your profits each year, after living expenses. The total (savings per year multiplied by the number of years to your planned exit) will be the right-hand base point of your triangle.

The triangle's base shows how far you can get towards the financial goals combining what you have now, and what the business should add to that amount by the time you exit. The "extension" of the base, the space between that projected right-hand base point and your financial objective, is your "Distance to Goal." That is the amount you will need from transferring or selling your business in order to sustain your desired lifestyle.

"I always hoped retirement would look like this."

Once you have a concrete, objective appraisal of your business you should be prepared to determine what needs to change in the triangulation graph (if anything) in order to cover your Distance to Goal. It will also help you estimate and determine the time it will take for you to get there.

If your business has excellent cash flow, but still has challenges that make it difficult or impossible to sell for other reasons, that distance will have to be covered by the profits you can draw out of the company between now and your exit.

If you have the time and the ambition, you may be able to take lower personal compensation in the short term in order to invest in the business's growth. You would then rely on generating a larger lump sum when you leave.

Of course, you may decide that your exit date has to be extended. In many cases, owners I work with are surprised to find that their time frame can be *shortened*.

This is an area where many owners experience a great deal of personal conflict. Sometimes they want to get out quickly, but the company won't provide the finances they need unless it has a number of years of strong growth. They are unwilling to either put in more effort or delay their departure, but still believe that the reward for a life in the business should be the life they expect in retirement.

In those cases, it's my job as an objective professional to inform a business owner quite simply, "You can't get there from here." The sides of the triangle can't have gaps with a little note that says, "And here a miracle happens." If the triangle and the company's value don't reach the financial objective, one or more of the parameters has to change.

This realization is never pleasant, and meets with a lot of denial. A business owner has worked for 40 years to build a company that is worth $1 million and now, as he approaches 70 years old, announces a retirement plan that would require $3 million post-tax proceeds (or about a $5 million sale price) from the business. It is difficult to determine how that goal can be achieved in the time frame he's set.

If that same owner was 55 years old, the path to the desired financial goals could be plotted out over a ten year period. That's why we recommend starting the exit planning process long before you are "ready" to leave. Having a plan in place doesn't require that you implement it immediately, but it goes a long way to helping you figure out where you want to go and how you are going to get there.

It's unusual to completely fund retirement needs
without any proceeds from your business.

If your calculations show that you can maintain your target lifestyle by exiting right now without the proceeds from your business, congratulations! You've done a great job of building your company and taking care of your personal financial needs at the same time. For most of us, however, the business is going to have to contribute a substantial portion of the Distance to Goal.

Most owners are fairly realistic about both the value of their business, its ability to grow, and their expectations for retirement lifestyle. The ability to get there without realizing *anything* from the business is uncommon.

5.3 Preparing Yourself

When should you start working on your exit plan? The simple answer is "As soon as you first think about it."

If you are unhappy when you drive to work, have a tough time returning from vacation, or think "Same s**t different day," while sitting in your office, it's time to start planning. If you have key employees asking when they will attain ownership, it's time to start planning.

As uncomfortable as it might be to admit; if your sales or profits have been flat for three years or more, and you aren't enthusiastic about the effort needed to grow, it's time to start planning.

Moving Forward

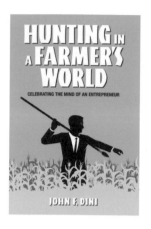

The first step in preparing to plan an exit is the most important. It is preparing yourself.

As I described at length in my previous book *Hunting in a Farmer's World*, the majority of business owners are Hunters. That means they are far better at moving towards a goal than the repetitive "farming" tasks of management. Most owners spend their careers focused on the next goal or the next challenge.

Hunters aren't very good at moving *away* from something. If you are waiting to plan until you can't stand running the company any longer, it will be too late. When I owned a business brokerage we'd say, "If an owner tells you that he or she is burned out, look at the financials. You'll see that he or she burned out three years ago." That almost always turned out to be the truth.

Burnout isn't the only reason an owner wants to sell immediately. Many such sales are driven by the "Dismal Ds."

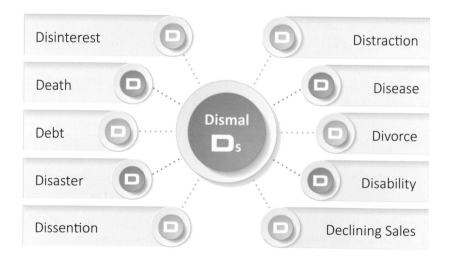

If you are trying to leave your business because of any one of the Dismal Ds, you are unlikely to develop a comprehensive exit plan.

The Dismal Ds are the reason behind many, and perhaps most, of the businesses that are brought to brokers. Perhaps that is one reason why 4 out of every 5 businesses listed by brokers fail to sell.

Even if you have the time and inclination to execute a planned exit strategy, there is still one obstacle. You'll need to develop a clear idea of where you will wind up after the business.

A successful exit requires that you are moving towards, not away from something.

I've tried to work with owners who say, "Let me get rid of the company, then I'll decide what comes next." It doesn't work. The closer they got to their exit, the more problems they found with the plan. In truth, they were just frightened of a world where they weren't business owners.

Ownership is part of your persona. It is how you are identified by family, friends, colleagues and competitors. Your life will be different after you give up what was your primary activity over the last 20, 30 or 40 years. I've heard more than a few times, "I never thought I'd get tired of playing golf."

Take some time to seriously consider how you will spend your days. It is more important than thinking about how you will spend your proceeds from exiting, although obviously the two are intertwined. We offer here (and in a fillable version on the website) a Personal Vision Worksheet that we've used with business owners for years. It doesn't cover everything, but it's a good start.

Personal Vision Worksheet©

An exit planning tool used to identify what you
want your business to do for you.

Name: _____

Date: _____

As an owner, you run a company for your own benefit. You assume the risks, and put in the effort, with an expectation of results. Clearly defining that objective helps keep your focus and balance.

Although developing a Personal Vison can be a done as an independent exercise by any business owner, we recommend utilizing this worksheet and working with a trusted advisor who can help you identify your goals.

Note: After completing the worksheet, you will be able to draft the final version of your Personal Vision which you should limit to <u>100 words</u>. You'll find that the discipline of making it short will help identify those things which are most important.

To start, please answer the following questions:

1. If your company was running "right," what would your job look like?

    Days and hours you would work: _____
    A typical day's activities: _____
    How much vacation would you take (<u>no contact</u> with business): _____

2. What material assets do you desire? (home, vacation home, cars, boats, etc.) List them and your estimate of the cost for each:

Asset:	Cost of Asset:
_____	$ _____
_____	$ _____
_____	$ _____
_____	$ _____
_____	$ _____

3. If you wish to travel, where, for what purpose, when and how long? _____

_____
_____
_____
_____

4. If you retire debt-free, what monthly/annual income is needed for your desired lifestyle?

Food and daily living: $ _____

Travel: $ _____

Hobbies, Sports, Interests: $ _____

Charity, Community: $ _____

Other: $ _____

Other: $ _____

Income providing capital (at 5%): $ _____

5. What non-material things attract you?

☐ Family
☐ Community
☐ Church
☐ Self-development
☐ Other: _____

6. When you retire, how will you spend your time? What are you doing now to prepare for that?

_____
_____
_____
_____
_____

7. Your Personal Vision "Balance Sheet"

	Current:	Goal:
Working Hours/Week:	_____	_____
Vacation Time:	_____	_____
Liquid Assets:	$_____	$_____
Major Assets:	$_____	$_____
Living Expenses:	$_____	$_____
Company Value at Sale:	$_____	$_____

Your Personal Vision calls for income in excess of living expenses over the next _____ years of $_____ in current dollars. How can that be achieved, while reaching your personal time and development targets? _____

_____
_____
_____
_____
_____

Focus on what you want to get out of your business, and when, with the Personal Vision Tool© at **www.YourExitMap.com.**

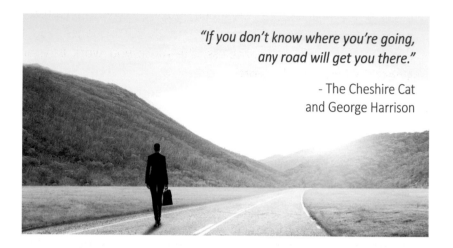

"If you don't know where you're going, any road will get you there."

- The Cheshire Cat
and George Harrison

You founded or acquired your business for a reason. If you are planning your exit, that objective either has been accomplished, will be accomplished, or can't be accomplished. Regardless of the reason for your exit, it will be far more difficult to execute if you don't know what comes next.

Emotional Detachment

Business owners live in, with and for their businesses. The absence of the daily stimulation of decision making, crises averted and small victories can leave a substantial emotional vacuum.

The time to begin emotionally withdrawing from your business is as soon as you start planning. Make a list of your tasks and responsibilities and identify areas that can be delegated. Training subordinates to assume your roles not only helps prepare you for the transition, it makes your company more valuable to a buyer.

Identify areas that can be delgated with The Owner Centricity Worksheet© at **www.YourExitMap.com**.

There is, however, a limit to how much detachment you can afford. If stepping back is going to damage company performance, you'll have to take it slowly. Nonetheless, the more you work *in* your business the less it will be worth.

Learn to be comfortable with
having others make decisions

Being an owner offers multiple adrenalin shots every day. You are accustomed to having the final say. Your friends, colleagues and associates all know you as the head honcho. Get accustomed to letting others make decisions, and learn how to be who you are without having the *gravis* of the company attached to you.

Lifestyle or Legacy?

Your decision regarding a preferred exit path depends on your objectives. Perhaps your triangulation tells you that your goals are achievable, and your personal vision has you excited about the next step in life. You still have one major question to answer. "Are you more concerned with lifestyle, or legacy?"

If your objective is to maximize lifestyle for yourself and your family after transition, you will have a valuation-driven exit plan. The years between start and implementation will be focused on improved business value drivers such as customer diversity, economies of scale and product differentiation.

If your main goal is to see the business continue a legacy of serving the customers, employees and community in the way it has under your leadership, then your planning will shift accordingly. You may choose an internal sale to employees or family. Internal sales are best for preserving the culture of a business, but are seldom the most lucrative exit strategy.

Disclosure

The biggest issue you'll have with any exit plan, whether it's to sell to a third party or internal succession, is intrusion. Prepare yourself in advance for invasive questions where your gut reaction is, "None of your damn business!"

The third-party due diligence process is onerous. Whatever you share won't be enough, especially when attorneys get involved. Even if you choose an internal sale you can expect that employees will have legal representation.

There are two cardinal rules for providing information to buyers.

First, have it ready and right. Clean financial records, policies and procedures, contracts, inventory and asset lists are going to be reviewed. Avoid looking foolish by presenting outdated or erroneous information. "We don't own that machine any longer," "We don't do it that way anymore," or "We don't close out those accounts until a month or two after the period ends," makes every other piece of information you submit suspect.

Second, address issues up front. It's far better to point out the loss of a major customer or key employee before the buyer discovers it. Sharing the information up front allows you to control the presentation. Doing it reactively never carries the same credibility.

Prepare for areas that need improvement with the Due Diligence Checklist© at **www.YourExitMap.com**.

You may want to consider an online repository for your documents, especially if you think they will be needed by multiple prospective buyers. There are many sites that allow contents to be released by level of authorization or only to specific users.

**Consider placing due diligence information
in a secure online repository.**

Many owners have told me that their first time through the due diligence process was highly educational. Even if the discussion doesn't result in a sale, learning what buyers want, and what concerns them, helps you be better prepared for the next discussion.

Life After the Business

Changing the habits of a lifetime isn't like throwing a switch. There are as many stories about owners who were miserable after exiting as there are about those who were happy.

My friend Allen Fishman, Founder of The Alternative Board®, tells a story about an owner who, in preparation for the sale of his business, spent $100,000 to build a woodworking shop behind his house.

Unfortunately, the man had never actually done any woodworking. It had always been a part of his Personal Vision; to have a woodworking shop where he could turn out beautiful furniture with no pressure from customers or employees.

You can probably guess what happened. After a couple of weeks staring at his woodworking equipment, he sold it all and bought another business. He was ready to exit, but he wasn't ready to stop doing what he enjoyed most; running an organization.

The Boomers not only have longer life expectancies than previous generations, their quality of life after 60 has improved dramatically. Most of us don't exclusively eat healthy food, and we fail to go to the gym often enough. Nonetheless, even our less-than-dedicated efforts, combined with vast improvements in medical care, have had a long term impact.

People now discuss "second careers" without fielding questions as to what that means. Charities and community service organizations are staffed with active and capable volunteers in their 60s, 70s and even into their 80s.

Exiting your business can mean a lot of things besides "retirement." But don't make the mistake of the woodworking shop owner. Decide on something you like, and try it out *before* you leave the business.

Family Businesses

The dynamics of family, both in and outside a business, fill many books. This particular book focuses on your exit planning options as a broad topic, but we'd be remiss if we didn't note the special issues of a family business.

We define a family business as any that has at least two generations actively working in the company.

We define a family business as any that has at least two generations actively working in the company. Either generation can be represented by multiple people. Two brothers and their sons, for example. Two brothers and the son of one of them. A mother and father with a daughter, or a father with three children. The dynamics are very different for each of those scenarios, as they are for scores of others.

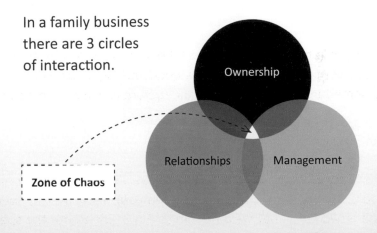

In a family business there are 3 circles of interaction.

Ownership

Relationships

Management

Zone of Chaos

1. **Ownership:** Who controls the stock or partnership interests? This is the level on which the final decisions are made, and the one where we do the most work in exit planning.

2. **Management:** Who makes the decisions for the business on a day to day basis?

3. **Relationships:** Are there employees who are siblings, offspring, or related by marriage? Is there more than one family unit involved? Are there children both in and outside the business? Are there step-children, or children from more than one marriage in the business?

Tales from the Trenches

Mike Cude

Michael Cude built Cude Engineers from a one-man shop to a firm of 92 civil engineering and surveying professionals. After his 60th birthday, Mike decided to begin planning a transition to his two sons (both engineers).

As the Great Recession slammed the construction market, the strain of downsizing the company and a serious illness impacted Mike's relationships. Eventually, his non-family partner and two employees formed a competitor. Mike's wife and partner in the business filed for divorce, and one of his sons left the company. His younger son bought the business.

Mike continues to work as a part time employee and 1% owner of Cude Engineers while pursuing outside consulting work and development in the storage business.

Life Intervenes

People ask me why I sold. I was just worn out. The recession, the divorce, the family infighting and my cancer all combined to make running the business a distraction, or perhaps the business was distracting me from my life. Either way, continuing as we were was untenable.

I made up my mind on the first day after the sale that I would continue to help and be supportive of my son as the new company leader. Once the skirmishing was done it became a lot easier. My son has done an excellent job of growing the business again, and we jointly own our new building. The rent is my best single income stream.

I enjoy what I do now more than I did running the business. I have more freedom. I spend some time as a consulting engineer for developers, and do some development of my own. My son is a partner in those projects. He runs the engineering company and I run the land company.

I wasn't ready to give up control. I enjoyed being a benevolent dictator. Everyone around me was frustrated however.

We were spending a lot of money on non-business related expenses, and it was no fun. If I had it to do again, I'm sure I would do some things differently. All in all, however, it came out okay.

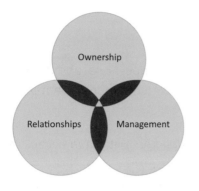 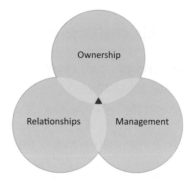

Where any two functions overlap, there is opportunity for friction.

Where all three overlap, there is the potential for chaos.

I am surprised at how often parents, realizing that the business is their largest single asset, decide to leave equal shares in it to all their children, whether they work in the company or not.

No matter how much siblings love each other, there is little chance that any of them will volunteer for a lifetime of working to enrich the others.

Consider having the non-active children commit to a sale contract upon inheritance. Their siblings can buy them out over time. This approach gives each child an equal share to start, but allows the working children to reap the benefits of building the company.

It feels a bit odd to offer only one strategy for this specific situation, no matter how often it occurs. When it comes to family business, we could add a hundred additional specific strategies and still not provide the one that applies to your situation. We just present this example to show that an inheritance plan can be fair and equitable without just "splitting the business up."

Consider having the non-active siblings
commit to a sale contract upon inheritance.

5.4 Along the Way

Your triangulation exercise will answer questions about where you are going and when you can expect to get there. The next key question is, "How?"

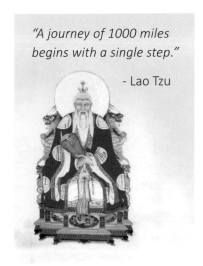

"A journey of 1000 miles begins with a single step."

- Lao Tzu

A qualified exit planner can help you determine whether a sale to a third-party or an internal transfer of the business to family or employees is a better option for you. Regardless of the road you choose, your employees are going to be a key component of your success. One solution is to make them the buyers. Another is to make them excited about helping you find a third party to take your place.

Employees as Buyers

If you are planning to offer your employees a leveraged buyout (LBO) or an Employee Stock Ownership Program (ESOP), their importance in the process is obvious. Unless you want to hold a note for the entire purchase price personally, (an approach I strongly discourage), your key employee team should be carefully vetted to determine their eligibility regarding management talent, ownership skills, and financial soundness.

Most planners use the Small Business Administration's (SBA) standards to judge financing qualifications. Many times a loan from a local bank without the government SBA guarantee is easier to arrange, but the SBA standards are consistent across the country. They have three major components.

National Small Business Administration
Loan Guarantee Key Criteria

(commercial lenders may have different or additional requirements)

---

 1. Equity: Generally speaking, buyers are expected to contribute 20% of the purchase price for a business, and at least 25% if they want to avoid encumbering their homes. The SBA will recognize existing equity as down payment. "Equity" in SBA parlance means stock the employees already own, or even stock they haven't paid for, but for which the seller is willing to hold a subordinated note.

 2. Management Skills: The most often neglected area of qualification is management skills. Unless the transition of responsibilities has been documented through the transition period, expect a lender to require the continued employment of the seller, or additional subordinated debt.

 3. Debt Service: The usual minimum acceptable coverage ratio is a history of generating $1.25 in free cash flow to every $1.00 of loan payments (5:4 ratio).

Stay Bonuses

If your strategy calls for sale to a third-party, your key employees can be a major influence not only in the salability of the company, but also in the probability of a smooth transfer after sale.

> Securing key employees post-sale commitment
> is a major factor in a sale.

Begin by designing retention bonuses to amply reward the employees who will help you reach the goal. These may take the form of stock appreciation rights, phantom stock or other virtual equity, "stay" bonuses, or another variant of a nonqualified deferred compensation (NQDC) plan. In any case, it should offer a suitable reward to the employee upon the execution of a successful transfer.

We can't overemphasize the importance of tying in your key employees to this kind of conditional compensation. It is not only motivational when focusing on growth initiatives before a sale, but it will prevent possible employee blackmail when a sale is imminent. There are many horror stories from the exit planning industry involving employees when no such reward was in place. Some are certainly apocryphal, but they all go something like this:

Brad Johnstone had worked long and hard to get a decent price for Legacy Fasteners Inc. The buyer's due diligence had been brutal, but now Brad was only a few days from executing a sale to Continental Industries.

As agreed, Continental had deposited the purchase price in escrow pending the official closing. Once they made that deposit, they had the right to talk with certain key employees who were not previously informed of the impending transaction. They came to visit Brad in his offices, and then used the conference room to interview a few people. One of these was Brad's sales manager, Jason Elmendorf.

A few minutes after the Continental folks left, Jason knocked on Brad's office door. "You have a minute Brad?" Brad invited him to come in and sit down.

"Those Continental Industry folks seem really nice," Jason said "They said that everyone's going to keep their jobs, and that they were particularly interested in having me continue. They told me that they paid almost $10 million for this company, and a large portion of it is due to the quality of its management."

"Since I am obviously a key factor in you getting this really large paycheck, Brad, I was wondering exactly how much of it you plan to share with me."

This isn't far-fetched. In fact, I've heard variations of the story repeated from coast-to-coast. In a transaction of the size described above, payouts to the Jasons of the world to keep the deal on track have ranged anywhere from $100,000 to $1,000,000. Typically, the amount involved is a lot more than what it would have cost to put incentives in place before the price of the company was negotiated.

5.5 Growth Strategies

Perhaps your strategy calls for growing the company, either to generate increased income for yourself, or for a higher price when it comes time to sell. (Actually, a growth strategy usually accomplishes both goals.)

Growth strategies can increase current income
or build value for a sale.

For many owners, the need for an elongated timeframe to accomplish their financial goals comes as an unpleasant surprise. They are unprepared to work for five years when they were planning to be gone in three, or stick around for ten years when they wanted to leave in five.

Few owners have a secret file of great ideas that they can access at will in order to improve their companies. They've already contributed everything they know. If your plan requires a long-term growth strategy, you may want to consider hiring someone who can add specific experience to your team.

Examine drivers that affect the value of your business with a free Assessment© at **www.YourExitMap.com.**

Value Drivers

Start by doing an honest assessment of the value drivers for your business. The Assessment at www.YourExitMap.com is free, takes only 15 minutes, and analyzes four key areas of your business.

Finance: How well your company fares against others in the industry, its market value, likely buyer segments, your personal credit support and tax implications.

Operations: Your contribution to daily operations, employee retention, management development, culture and systems.

Revenue/Profit trends: Customer concentration, margins, sales and product differentiation.

Planning: Emergency contingencies and succession, retirement needs, transfer mechanisms, post-exit preparedness.

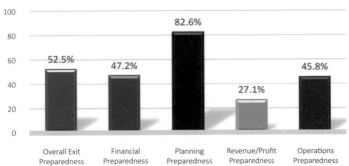

Exit Preparedness Snapshot

- Overall Exit Preparedness: 52.5%
- Financial Preparedness: 47.2%
- Planning Preparedness: 82.6%
- Revenue/Profit Preparedness: 27.1%
- Operations Preparedness: 45.8%

Strategic Growth Systems

This is not an organizational development book. It is intended to enlighten, entertain and inform, but not to give you a specific step-by-step process for improving your company.

A business growth consultant can lead you through an organized planning system, and help hold you and your team accountable for the results. A good consultant will help you develop KPI's (Key Performance Indicators) and tracking metrics to determine whether you are on course to achieve your ultimate goal.

Since an exit plan is, by its very nature, a strategic plan; some growth consultants include exit planning as part of their practices, but most focus on operational and bottom-line improvement.

> Choosing the system is not nearly as important
> as choosing the consultant.

There are many growth planning systems on the market. I am familiar with a few that I think work well in privately held companies. Choosing the system is not nearly as important as choosing the consultant. Find someone who is both pleasant to work with and strong enough to stand up to you if you begin backsliding.

Be wary of someone who offers to design "whatever you want," and implement "however you want." They are probably not going to be of great help if your exit plan calls for reaching a new level of profitability. A growth consultant should be challenging your ideas of what can be accomplished and stretching your goals.

All the systems I recommend have professionals certified in their use around the United States. You can contact any of them for the names of qualified practitioners in your area.

Systems I've worked with, or seen used with positive effects include (in alphabetical order):

EOS	Gazelles	VBS
by Gino Wickman	*by Verne Harnish*	*by John Warrillow*

- **EOS:** The Entrepreneurial Operating System, created by Gino Wickman and outlined in the book *Traction*, is a system that seems to work especially well in smaller companies that have never used an organized planning system. It takes pieces from several other approaches, and combines them in a fairly simple and easy to follow format. It focuses on accountability and execution in a management team. As such, it is an excellent approach when internal buyers need to "step up their game" as future owners.

- **Gazelles:** Originally developed from the ideas in Verne Harnish's excellent book *Mastering the Rockefeller Habits*, Gazelles is a comprehensive system of online forms and support. It is outlined in Verne's new book *Scaling Up*. I have found Gazelles to be appropriate for fast-growing companies, technology based businesses, and those that seek to outgrow the neutral zone (too small to be big, but too big to be small).

- **VBS:** The Value Builder System grew out of John Warrillow's book *Built to Sell*. John has done an excellent job of measuring the impact of rising scores in the VBS assessments and correlating them to increases in valuation multiples at sale. This approach is more focused on business metrics rather than the personal objectives focus of exit planning, but many exit planners include VBS as part of their offerings.

An exit plan is a strategy
with an end date.

One of the big advantages of working on growth strategies with a business owner who has developed his or her exit strategy is the concept of a deadline. The projected exit date becomes a concrete goalpost that is the objective of the entire game plan.

This creates a certain urgency with both the owner and the key employees. For that reason, growth strategies in preparation for exiting tend to be better structured and adhered to than in situations where growth would merely be "nice."

Acquisitions

Another viable growth strategy, and one too often ignored by smaller business, is acquisition.

Buying a company isn't only for financial wizards. If you are among the younger half of the Boomers (born between 1955 and 1964), you have plenty of time to build up your value by purchasing other companies in the same or complementary market space.

Acquisition strategies
aren't just for financial wizards.

Your targets will be companies owned by older Boomers and the WWII generation. As many of these owners find limited avenues to a profitable exit, you can step in. The best scenario for you as a buyer will be to use as little cash as possible, and let the acquired company pay for itself.

There are a number of ways to structure low - or no - cash acquisitions:

Earn Outs

Most common in service industries, this is where you purchase the customer base of a company. In return, you promise to pay a certain percentage of the revenues generated from those customers over a period of time. The seller is motivated to assist in a smooth transition, in return for a few years of continued income without running the company

Consulting Agreements

These can be used in either service or product based businesses. The buyer acquires the assets of the company at book value. The seller then receives a salary, retainer of commissions for a specific length of time, usually in return for continuing service to his or her customer base.

Ride Alongs

If you are acquiring a business as a component of a comprehensive plan to sell, you can leave a non-controlling interest with the seller, who hopes to profit from your eventual "flip" of the consolidated businesses. This is especially effective when the transaction will put the buyer in a higher-multiple strata of eventual acquirers. The original seller then stands to benefit from the arbitrage of his company's value.

Tales from the Trenches

David Spencer

David left his government engineering job for a successful bid on a retrofitting contract for the United States Air Force. On Board Software's performance on that program and those that followed built a fast growing technology company. David, however, felt that further expansion would require more than his own personal relationships. He began seeking a strategic partner with broader access to opportunities.

David decision to sell the entire business was lucrative, but more importantly was influenced by his four-year earn out contract for leveraging On Board's capabilities into the new owners customer base. Unfortunately, such development required shared incentives, and David found out that his corporate superiors had compensation packages driven by their existing model of cost cutting and expense control, instead of overall profitability which would support his earn out.

David resigned four months into his four year agreement.

Culture Club

One of the things I didn't anticipate about the transaction was its impact on our business development bow wave. Due diligence was brutal, and it was a distraction from continuing to chase new business. I think eventually we reached a point of no return, where if we didn't follow through on the deal, the damage to the businesses in lost opportunity would have been considerable.

I had a mentor who ran his own company. He gave up almost nine months of his life to help me through the transaction, and in the end wouldn't take a cent for it. (I did donate a large check for his church's building fund in his name, which he didn't turn down.)

I wanted my employees to know how important they were in the process. The day after closing, I gave out over $8 million in bonuses. They were distributed strictly by seniority, so a few administrative workers received more than some executives. Many told me how those checks had changed their lives.

Unfortunately, none of the anticipated job growth from the acquisition occurred. The cost-cutting culture not only drove me away, it likely tanked two more acquisitions for that company. All the executives to whom I reported were gone within two years, and what was left of On Board Software got parsed out to a new acquirer when our acquiring company was sold for one-fifth of their previous market value.

The money gave me freedom to give back as a philanthropist and public servant. I spent three years as the inaugural Chair of the Texas Emerging Technology Fund, and continue to devote substantial time and money working with our local university in building their science and technology programs. For a while I was a full time technology investor, but couldn't escape my entrepreneurial bug and have built a new company that is developing medical devices for the military. I also helped found two banks.

5.6 Third-Party Buyer Design

If you plan on transitioning your business via a sale to a third party, it can pay handsomely if you do a little homework. Design your growth strategy to focus on the features found most attractive to your target buyers. A short video on buyers and the multiples they customarily pay is available on <u>www.YourExitMap.com</u>.

Main Street Entrepreneurs

If you are selling a Main Street (under $3,000,000 value) business to an individual buyer, he or she will most appreciate strong cash flow (measured as Seller's Discretionary Earnings), and predictable profitability. It also helps if your business has substantial assets to act as collateral for financing.

> **Long-term growth strategies should be designed
> with a specific class of buyer in mind.**

Remember, although you may take considerable perks from your business, many (such as pocketed cash or bartered services) will not count when a lender looks at financial statements. Make sure you show sufficient profitability to qualify for financing, if such will be necessary.

*My first book **11 Things You Absolutely Need to Know about Selling Your Business**, is a step-by-step look at exiting a Main Street (under $3,000,000 valuation) business by listing it with a broker for third-party sale. It's a nuts and bolts book, used by many business brokers to help their clients prepare for the process.*

Industry Buyers

If you are selling to a competitor, internal systems and upper management will be less of a factor than if you are selling to an unrelated third party. A competitor will be more interested in the quality of your customer base from the perspective of gross sales, customer concentration, and collectability of the accounts receivable.

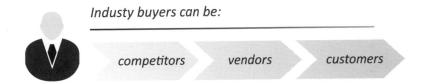

Industy buyers can be:

competitors   vendors   customers

Selling to a competitor requires a very careful approach to sharing information. We'll discuss confidentiality in just a moment.

Professional Investors

The financial buyer, such as a private equity group or a family office, is all about cash flow. They are seeking a specific return on investment and want an acquisition that will appeal to their investors. Expect them to be challenging when negotiating price, especially if they ask for a "quality of earnings" audit.

Professional investors focus on
acquisitions that appeal to their investors.

Financial buyers also place a premium on a strong management team that can function without the seller, since they seldom bring industry-specific management talent as part of the deal. If you are targeting this group, pay special attention to your key employee retention strategy.

Strategic Buyers

Strategic buyers are usually more interested in revenue growth. It is a better indicator that the company can be scaled to the volumes they anticipate after acquisition. Although increasing profitability is nice, they'll frequently sacrifice it for impressive topline results.

Remember, publicly-traded strategic buyers are frequently going to add your profits to an annual report where they are already valued at 12 to 20 times earnings. That's why strategic buyers pay such attractive multiples. They benefit from the arbitrage opportunity of paying 7, 8, or even 10 times earnings, which are then automatically enhanced on their next annual report.

5.7 Internal Sales

There are several reasons why owners consider an internal transition. Sales to insiders may be driven by family considerations, a desire to see the owner's legacy continued, or financial objectives.

Selling to insiders is a more relaxed process. Valuation is often a lesser concern. (Note: If you want to maximize every penny from your business as a matter of pride, a third-party sale is more likely to accomplish that.) Owners frequently value the business more as a factor in their retirement goals than strictly considering Fair Market Value.

**In an internal sale, both buyer and seller
are motivated to increase value.**

Time frames may be more flexible, due diligence is less exhausting, and if structured properly, both buyer and seller are highly motivated to cooperate in activities focused on increasing value. This is often accomplished by allowing employees to become owners gradually.

Seller-Financed Internal Sale

Profits

owner → note from buyers → installment payments →

─ ─ ─ owner in control ─ ─ ─ ─ ─ owner at risk ─ →

Planned Transition Internal Sale (LBO)

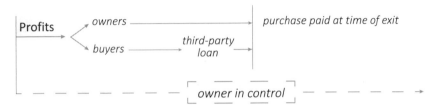

Profits

owners ──────────── purchase paid at time of exit

buyers ──────── third-party loan →

─ ─ ─ ─ ─ ─ ─ owner in control ─ ─ ─ ─ →

Leveraged Buyouts

When we bring up the possibility of selling to employees, an owner usually says something like, "Sure, I have good managers who could run this business, but they have no money."

Enter the Leveraged Buyout (LBO). The LBO is a process whereby key employees in the business use the cash flow of the company to underwrite its purchase.

If you stop to think about it, the cash flow of a business is *always* the source of funding for a sale anyway. If a buyer pays cash, he or she expects the company to provide a return on that investment.

Similarly, if the buyer borrows money from a bank, the loan committee is going to approve financing based on the company's ability to finance the debt.

The simplest type of LBO is when an owner sells to the employees for a promissory note. Unfortunately, that can often lead to one of two scenarios.

 Micromanagement: The seller sees to the security of his financing by remaining engaged with the business. Not only has the owner "failed" the exit plan, but the new owners are denied the opportunity to learn for themselves. After a while, they may want to consider hiring a hit man to make the former owner go away.

 Benign Neglect: In these cases, the seller watches over the business for a few months or a few quarters. When things seem to be going smoothly, he stops watching. Then a rude awakening comes when the payments stop. That's when the seller discovers that the employees have hit hard times, or mismanaged the business. Unfortunately, the seller's only recourse at that point is to take back the broken business and try to fix it. Clearly, that isn't why he exited in the first place.

We prefer a modified LBO structure in which the seller maintains control of the business until his proceeds are securely in his pocket.

*Internal sales should be structured
so that the owner retains control until he is paid.*

In these cases, the owner sells stock incrementally to the employees over several years. As their ownership increases, they use their share of the profits to pay for their stock. When they've amassed sufficient equity to qualify for a loan (most lenders consider ownership to be the equivalent of a "down payment"), they finance (leverage) the rest of the purchase through a bank.

Many owners say, "Wait a minute. They are buying the company with *my* money." That is true, but you have to consider two facts:

1. All acquisitions are paid for with the cash flow of the acquired business. You are simply frontloading the (smaller) installment note portion so you can get the (larger) cash portion when you leave.

2. You remain in control of the time, price and method of your exit until you have the proceeds in hand.

Employee Ownership Incentives

When planning a leveraged buyout, employees will usually earn the right to purchase equity by achieving certain growth objectives in the business. Reaching these growth objectives helps you achieve your financial targets while also proving lucrative to your employees.

This is one of the most rewarding examples of the whole being greater than the sum of its parts. Highly motivated employees not only step up to relieve the owner of responsibilities, but simultaneously try to increase the value of the organization. The more they increase the value of the owner's equity, the more valuable their own holdings become.

Partial sales to employees are still beneficial if a company is eventually purchased by a third party, because their equity can also be structured as a retention incentive.

ESOP

When people mention a sale to employees, many advisors respond with, "Oh, you mean an ESOP." Employee Stock Ownership Plans are a specific, federally-regulated method of internal sale. They aren't for everyone, but under the right circumstances an ESOP can be a lucrative strategy for both the buyers and seller.

ESOPs are ERISA-compliant plans. That means they, like a 401k or an IRA, have to be open to all employees. However, they also provide a few huge advantages to the seller.

Like ERISA-compliant plans, ESOPs pay no taxes. This offers substantial advantages when using the ESOP's share of the profits to pay down the purchase financing.

A second advantage to the seller is that, under certain circumstances, the proceeds from a sale can be reinvested in publicly traded securities, and tax is deferred until the portfolio is liquidated. The ability to invest 100% of the sale price means that the principal amount can grow substantially.

ESOP Cash Flow
(Illustration After a Subchapter S Election)

Of course, no government-designed program is without its drawbacks. ESOPs are expensive to establish. I've not seen any implemented for much less than $250,000, and some cost much more.

Employee Stock Ownership Plans
have substantial regulatory requirements.

There are also requirements for outside directors, audited financial statements and regular third-party valuations. Those annual maintenance costs are usually between $50,000 and $100,000. For that reason, we seldom see or recommend ESOPs in companies with annual revenues below $10,000,000.

Hybrid Buyouts

Most owners want the company to be managed well after they move on. They cringe at the thought of an employee democracy making decisions. A common misconception is that since an ESOP must encompass all employees, it must also include direct employee control of the business.

That is not the case. An ESOP can own anything from a small percentage to complete control of an entity. Key employees can also have additional ownership outside the ESOP. Properly structured, these key employees can have *de facto* control of the business decisions while the seller still enjoys some of the ESOP's benefits.

Owners considering an ESOP may have nightmares about employee votes on major business issues. That isn't a problem. An ESOP is treated like a single shareholder. It functions similarly to a 401K, where employees enter and exit the plan under pre-set conditions. That means other shareholders outside of the plan can still control decisions regarding operational issues.

Family Succession

Internal transitions to family members involve a different set of motivations. The value of the business is usually considered part of the owner's estate. Planning often includes consideration of siblings both in and outside the company.

In family succession, tax planning often supersedes an arms-length business valuation. Unfortunately, many family businesses try a do-it-yourself approach to planning. Dad (or Mom) says "This is the way I see it. I built this business. I figured out how you will pay for it, and you are lucky to get it."

Just because there is no argument doesn't mean it's the best plan. Please don't attempt a family succession without at least retaining a good tax advisor.

Hard to Sell Companies

Certain types of businesses are poor candidates for third party buyers, but work very well as internal sales. An example of such a business is a construction company that bids for work. Third party buyers are reluctant to pay for any business that is only as successful as its next estimate, and in which a poorly run job can sink the company.

New competitors seldom need the overhead of an existing staff. They can just start bidding jobs and hire personnel when needed.

Because of these factors, owners of construction companies or similar businesses frequently face difficulty in finding a buyer. Often closing down appears to be the only exit possibility. Employees, however, are accustomed to bidding for work. They share key relationships, and know that they are able to run jobs at a profit. Properly "constructed," the exit plan for such a company can offer both Fair Market Value to its owner and a terrific opportunity to its employees.

5.8 The Art of the Deal

With no apologies to Mr. Trump, there is art in other deals besides real estate. Exit plans always result in a transaction, which indicates that there is a buyer (employees, family or third party) and a seller. That means there is a deal to be structured.

In every transaction, certain elements remain constant. We describe a third party transaction here. The same elements exist in an internal sale, but they are more apt to be part of a cooperative effort between the buyer(s) and seller.

"Just to get the negotiation off on the right foot, I don't intend to concede anything."

Tales from the Trenches

Arnold Goldman

Arnold is an experienced serial entrepreneur. He built a multi-location retail chain in New Your City. When he sold that, he relocated to Florida where he purchased a window tinting distribution business. While the company grew five fold in the first five years, he discovered that his partner was not managing the company funds prudently. Angry and frustrated, Arnold confronted him and gave him a choice. He placed a value on the business and told his partner to choose between being the buyer or the seller.

The partner chose to buy the business, and Arnold invested the proceeds in a roofing company. In the next decade he grew revenues tenfold, but again began seeking a better opportunity. A representative of a private equity group had examined the company as a potential platform for a roll up. When that didn't materialize, he presented himself as a buyer.

Trust, but Verify

Like most people who have experience in the financial industry, the buyer offered me a deal structure that involved extended financing and handcuffs for me. He put 50% down in cash, with a five year note for the balance. I had an employment contract as a salesman, with no required hours and an easily achievable quota.

In the first year I sold a roofing job for three times my annual quota. The new owner promptly fired me, and refused to pay the commission. Shortly after that, the payments on the note stopped.

My experience taught me to make sure any note was secured, and I had gotten the buyer's personal guaranty, as well as placing a lien on his commercial property holdings. I sued for the note balance and the commission. Eventually I won both, but only after two years of fighting.

I spent a long time during the litigation in a state of depression. Although I won, it was hard to do anything else during that period and for many years after. I'm now a coach and consultant to business owners. I think a large part of my value comes from my clients learning about my mistakes and my penchant for asking "But what if...?"

The Standard Elements of a Transaction

Price

Due Dilligence

Transition

Post-Closing

Handcuffs

Price

In a third party sale, negotiation encompasses everything from price to financing, and from the timing of announcements to contact with your employees.

The price in a Letter of Intent (LOI)
may be far different from what is actually paid.

Many sellers make the mistake of concentrating on price as the first priority in a negotiation. Other factors can dramatically impact your post-tax proceeds, including:

• Whether it is a stock or an asset sale ⟶
(Available at www.YourExitMap.com)

• Assignment of certain classes of assets and your basis in them

• Price reductions for customer concentration or employment liabilities

Due Diligence

Expect a buyer to look carefully at the quality of your earnings. Many initial offers are later reduced for risk factors. Each of these may require separate negotiations.

- Customer concentration

- Employment liabilities

- Future service agreement obligations

- Stale accounts receivable

- Obsolete inventory

- Technology shifts in an industry (disruptors)

Stock Sales vs. Asset Sales

Item	Stock Sale	Asset Sale
Seller's Tax Liability	Capital gains tax	Ordinary income tax (possible alternative minimum tax)
Buyer's Tax Basis	Price of stock	Price of assets
Seller's Treatment of Intangible Assets	N/A	May be eligible for capital gains treatment if held personally outside the entity, otherwise ordinary income
Seller's Treatment of Tangible Assets	N/A	If sale price exceeds book value, ordinary income tax is due on "overpayment"
Buyer's treatment of Intangible Assets	N/A, part of basis	15-year depreciation
Buyer's Treatment of Tangible Assets	N/A, part of basis	New depreciation schedules begin at the time of sale with the amount paid
Seller's Legal Liability	Technically ends with transfer of the entity	Remains with owner of entity at time of incident; no transfer of liability
Buyer's Legal Liability	Assumes responsibility for past actions of the entity	Acquiring entity starts with clean slate

Transition

Almost inevitably, you will be expected to continue working as an employee through some transition period. Negotiate your post-sale employment agreement just as you would any other business transaction.

- Is your compensation for transition work part of the sale price?

- What are the time limits on your required participation?

- Can you choose, limit or define your exact duties?

- Are extensions to the transition period available, and if so, on what terms?

- Are you incented for the company's performance during your transition tenure?

Post-Closing

There are as many ways to impact a price after closing as can be created by business attorneys. Here are a few of the more common issues you'll have to determine.

- Penalties for discrepancies in your representations and warranties

- "Claw-backs" for return of funds already remitted

- Escrow agreements to hold funds for a year or more for potential problems

- Minimum thresholds for single reimbursable events

- Aggregate thresholds for multiple reimbursable events

- Penalties for the buyer's failure to retain key employees

- Minimum time frames for customer retention

- Earn-outs requiring certain levels of future performance to earn contingency funds

Handcuffs

Buyers expect you to completely exit the industry, or to remain removed from it until they are sure you don't pose a competitive threat. Most transactions include some financial penalty for sellers who fail to live up to the letter of their commitments in a number of areas.

- Contact with former customers

- Communicating with or hiring former employees

- Working for another company in your industry, whether it's a former customer, vendor or competitor

5.9 Confidentiality

Planning your exit from a business is a process of telling secrets. For many owners, it is the most terrifying part of selling.

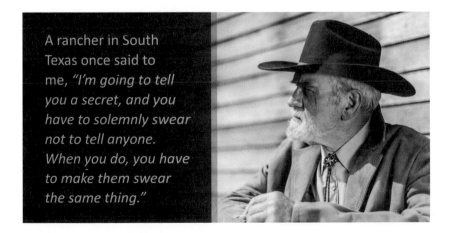

A rancher in South Texas once said to me, *"I'm going to tell you a secret, and you have to solemnly swear not to tell anyone. When you do, you have to make them swear the same thing."*

Most business owners are very cautious about with whom they share their exit plans. The logic is intuitive. The more the information is shared, the bigger the chance is that someone will use the knowledge against you.

Competitors will tell customers, insinuating that your company will no longer be a dependable supplier. Employees might begin looking for greater security in other jobs. Vendors may seek another distribution channel. Your bank could start tightening your credit.

Yet your buyer wants to verify due diligence information. He wants to talk to key employees and customers. Lines of supply and the solidity of relationships have to be confirmed.

Some owners are unduly afraid of letting anyone know their plans. Sooner or later everyone will know, but *when* they should be informed is an important part of your planning. Controlling the distribution of information might have dramatic impact on the value of your business.

Those who should know about your plans
can be placed in three different groups.

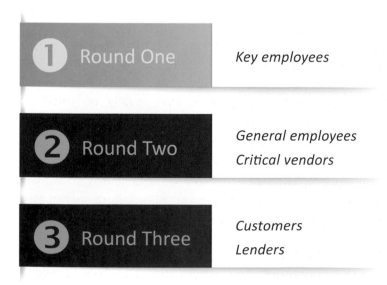

① Round One	*Key employees*
② Round Two	*General employees* *Critical vendors*
③ Round Three	*Customers* *Lenders*

Round One

> **Key employees:** Whether they are slated to be the next generation of owners or not, key employees should be the earliest group informed of your plans. Of course if you are contemplating an internal sale, their willingness and ability to buy the company requires disclosure. If you are planning an external sale, their cooperation in preparing the company for a buyer's due diligence will be critical.

Key employees should be among the first
informed of your exit planning.

Consider having the employees sign a new non-disclosure agreement. Even if you have confidentiality provisions in your employment contracts or policy manual, it serves to emphasize the sensitive nature of exit planning information.

Round Two

Going outside your trusted inner circle is a big step, but you should consider it once you have a solid buyer in place. Sharing earlier, rather than later, makes due diligence easier.

> **General employees:** Employees can usually be informed fairly early in the sale process. Explain that the transition of the company is a normal part of its lifecycle, and that you are taking steps to ensure that it is done with an eye to their continued employment. That will go a long way to making them feel more secure. If you treat it like a dark secret, they will have greater concerns about the inevitable rumors.

That's why I suggest you inform the employees before you tell vendors and competitors, from whom they are likely to hear it anyway. Bringing them "in the know" will also help forestall any hiring attempts by other businesses. Inertia is a powerful force. Usually after a few weeks with no major disruption, the employees just accept your exit planning as a fact of life.

Critical vendors: If you have an exclusive distribution or supply relationship with some larger companies you may already be fielding requests for a documented succession plan. Many suppliers appreciate the forethought of exit planning because it ensures the stability of their distribution chain.

One area of caution. Watch out for a vendor's loose lipped salespeople, who may regard news of your pending departure as hot gossip for the rest of their customers.

Round Three

Customers: Most customers should be told as late as possible before the transaction closes. If informed of a *fait accompli,* they are likely to stick with the relationship long enough to gain some experience with the new owners. If informed too far in advance, customers will logically begin to look for alternative sources of supply.

Lenders: While many bankers and other lenders will say that they ought to be informed as early as possible in the process, it is often not a great idea. They may seek the opportunity to finance a transaction, and certainly would like to begin a relationship with any new owner, but they also have a primary responsibility to protect the assets of their institution.

Bankers have to be concerned about the security of your personal guarantees, and whether there is any risk to their capital in your business. Discussions with your bank should include details about the future of your banking relationship.

Due diligence is only one step in the process of telling secrets. Lots of other stakeholders will need to be informed. How and when you do that should be a formal part of your planning process.

5.10 Building a Team

A successful transition requires the support of multiple professionals.

At a minimum your team should consist of:

- **Business Attorney:** Many attorneys can easily handle routine contracts for small businesses, but a good one will have a comprehensive knowledge of escrow agreements, chargebacks, and liability collars on your representations and warranties. In an internal sale, you want someone who is experienced in designing buy/sell and equity option agreements.

- **Certified Public Accountant:** Your tax preparer may or may not have the experience to render expertise in a transaction. Such practitioners need to be experienced in the special issues created when a company changes hands. Those may include taxation of inventory, depreciation recovery, taxation when exercising options or virtual equity rights, personal goodwill, and payment structure of the sale. It is also critical that they are experienced in taxation for your type of entity. Partnerships, corporations and LLCs pose very different challenges in planning.

- **Estate Attorney:** Your estate attorney has the job of protecting your assets following the sale, and in the event anything happens to make you incapable of completing the transition. This includes knowledge of wills, inheritance law, and a wide range of revocable, irrevocable and charitable trusts.

- **Exit Planner:** This person should probably be certified by one of the three certifying organizations in the United States, The Business Enterprise Institute, the Exit Planning Institute, or Pinnacle Equity Solutions, which is an indication that he or she is sufficiently aware of the implications inherent in a transition to coordinate the other, more technical professionals. Just as we recommend professionals with a special concentration in each technical area, exit planning skill does not come automatically with a degree in law, an accounting certification or a business broker's license. Your exit planner should be prepared to act as your coach, the quarterback of the planning team, and may also add a technical specialty of his or her own.

- **Financial Planner:** This person may or may not be a wealth manager, and may or may not sell insurance. The chief criteria is that they understand how to develop projections for a successful retirement, and are aware of the various types of risk mitigation instruments (insurance) that could be used to ensure the successful completion of your plan.

There are a few other professionals you may wish to consider either for one-time input or for a project to help implement your strategy. (See the glossary for specific titles and certifications.)

- **Business Appraiser or Valuation Specialist:** A professional who can deliver an objective, rational, defensible opinion of your company's value both for the purposes of the transaction and for documenting the logic of your tax treatment to the IRS. Look not only for credentials, but also for a track record in valuing businesses of your size or in your industry.

- **Business Growth Consultant:** A person who specializes in working with a management team to develop the skills necessary for assuming control of the business, and is practiced with objective measurements of an organization's success.

Tales from the Trenches

Randy Smith

Randy founded Forum Systems Group, and built it into a market-dominant provider of restaurant point of sale systems. As a member of the software company's Dealer Advisory Board, Randy worked with the organization's President, who agreed to acquire Forum Systems in order to bring Randy onto his executive team.

Unfortunately, in the middle of the transaction, the $800 million acquirer was itself bought by a $5 billion technology company. The executives whom Randy worked with were eliminated after the transaction, leaving Randy as the operator of a branch operation answering to middle management.

Swallowed by the Whale

I had reached a point where I felt my company had gone as far as it could under my leadership. I'd acquired and grown a second office in another state to prove that my systems were scalable, but I no longer wished to put in the time and energy required at the expense of my family.

Five years before the sale I'd started to build an organization that could run without me. I hired a business coach and joined a business owner peer group, both of which were invaluable in giving me objective feedback on the things I implemented.

I signed an employment contract with the acquirer. Although I knew that the original plan to join the executive team was no longer, I thought continuing to run my business would be much like when I owned it. That wasn't the case. I now reported to a boss who knew far less about our industry and our market than I did.

On the first day after leaving my positon at the acquiring company, I drove my daughters to school, just like every previous week day. After I dropped them off, I sat in the car wondering where to go next. After a few minutes I just turned around and went home. I took the next six months to reorganize my life and catch up on all the "deferred maintenance" that was always second fiddle to running the business.

Selling the company gave me a sense of accomplishment, and secured my familiy's financial future. As owners we are selfish. We sacrifice in the name of the business, and take risks that we justify while ignoring their impact on others. It took some time to understand that being an owner wasn't just about me.

5.11 Why Start an Exit Plan?

I've been a business owner for a long time. I understand why the thought of retaining six or seven professionals for one project can give someone the willies. Most of us aren't really practiced at reading tea leaves ten years in advance, either.

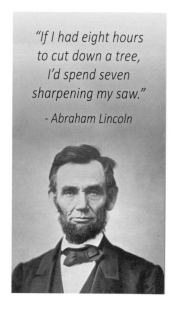

"If I had eight hours to cut down a tree, I'd spend seven sharpening my saw."

- Abraham Lincoln

One of our clients who owns eight restaurants recently asked me: "Have I lost my entrepreneurial nerve? I used to drive past a location I liked, and I'd have a restaurant there 60 days later. Now I take months and months to make the decision."

I, too, move slower on major business decisions, but I think it's just because I've grown more appreciative of advance planning.

Starting when you still have plenty of runway ahead helps. So does having one professional who manages the others (and keeps their billable hours in check). Technical specialists are most cost-effective when you've worked through your strategy prior to getting them involved.

Given clear direction, each one of the professionals listed can add thousands, and in some cases hundreds of thousands of dollars to your eventual proceeds.

Of course, the simplest answer to "Why" is

"Because it is probably the single biggest financial event of your life."

You are unlikely to get a second shot at it.

POST SCRIPT

Getting Started

Post Script

I hope that you enjoyed this book. I set out to provide readers with something that is more entertaining than the traditional "I'm a consultant, and here's what I think you should do" book. Of course you should be planning your exit, but I wanted you to know why it is more important than ever, and when (how long) your lead time should be.

I also wanted the book to be fun to read. Exiting should be fun. It is the culmination of a career, and it should feel like a crowning achievement. Some of the material is a bit dry, but we thought the pictures and color would at least brighten it up a bit.

Getting Started

If you are a Baby Boomer (or older) we've laid out a pretty strong case for planning your exit. The reasons are simple enough.

Why?

- It's likely going to be the biggest financial transaction of your life.

- The process can be complex and, depending on your strategy, can take a significant amount time.

- Future valuations will likely decline as a result of the limited number of qualified buyers.

- There will be many other businesses much like yours to choose from, and you need to make sure your company stands out from the rest.

When?

- As soon as you begin thinking about retirement.

- When work is no fun anymore.

- When you turn 55 years old (or sooner!).

- At least five years before you want to walk away. If you don't know when that is, start now.

If the reasons for planning your exit are this obvious, why have less than 25% of Boomer owners discussed exiting with their professional advisors? (Business Enterprise Institute – 2014) Why do 85% of owners regardless of age think they will sell to a third party in 5 years? (Price Waterhouse Coopers – 2008)

It's because Boomers, especially Boomer entrepreneurs, are what they do. They are no more anxious to discuss exiting than they are to start shopping around for a cemetery plot.

It's too bad, because the future of their families, their employees and their customers rests on their willingness to deal with an inescapable truth. Sooner or later, every owner leaves his or her business. You've worked hard to build a business. You should remain in control of the time, method and proceeds of your exit transition.

How?

1. Go to www.YourExitMap.com and take the free Assessment.

2. Bring the ExitMap® Assessment© report to your preferred professional advisor to discuss.

3. If you want a complete review, along with a 40 page response-by-response analysis, contact one of the qualified ExitMap® Affiliates listed on the site for a debriefing or encourage your own advisor to become a Qualified ExitMap® Affiliate.

4. Use the free tools on www.YourExitMap.com to test your assumptions about timeframes, retirement needs, valuation and objectives.

5. Read the free white papers on the site about the aspects of planning that apply to you.

6. Subscribe to www.awakeat2oclock.com for regular articles on the latest in exit planning trends, tools and strategies along with stories from other owners about their exits.

Ultimately, you will exit your business. You can either plan for the transition on your own terms, or you can just let it be a surprise!

John F. Dini

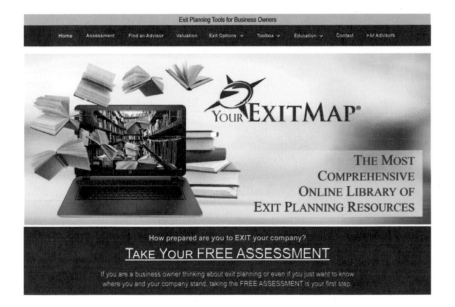

About the Author

John F. Dini CMBA, CExP
President, MPN Incorporated

John F. Dini is a consultant and coach to hundreds of business owners, CEOs and entrepreneurs, His book *Hunting in a Farmer's World: Celebrating the Mind of an Entrepreneur,* won "Best Business Book" at the New York Book Festival and the National Silver Medal for business books from the Independent Publishers' Association.

He is also the author of *Beating the Boomer Bust and 11 Things You Absolutely Need to Know About Selling Your Business,* now In its second edition. John holds a BS in Accounting from Rutgers University, and an MBA from Pepperdine University, along with six additional business certifications.

John writes numerous articles on exit strategy for newspapers, trade magazines, and in his own blog "Awake at 2 o'clock?" He is a 15-year member of Jim Blasingame's "Braintrust," appearing regularly on "The Small Business Advocate" nationally syndicated radio program, as an expert in the issues of business ownership. John also speaks to regional and national groups of business owners and their advisors.

The message of *Your Exit Map: Navigating the Boomer Bust* is available as a keynote presentation for business owners and their advisors. Please inquire through www.johnfdini.com.

John also takes a limited number of consulting engagements with mid-market companies investigating their options for internal transfer. www.mpninc.com.

You can subscribe to John Dini's blog about planning your exit at www.awakeat2oclock.com.

Interview Questions

For the "Interviews with Influencers" and "Tales from the Trenches" features in this book, the following questions were asked:

CEO Interview Questions

1 What changes, if any, do you anticipate in the landscape of entrepreneurship in the United States?

2 How is your industry preparing for the transition of the Baby Boomer workforce?

3 What is your company doing to facilitate or manage the exit of Boomer employees?

4 Do you think the number of businesses transferred to employees will increase (due to a lack of third party buyers) or decline (due to a lack of interest or lack of means)?

5 Baby Boomers, via their sheer numbers, the entry of women in the workforce and their competitiveness, drove the longest economic expansion in history. What will happen to the economy as they step down?

6 Small businesses face more regulation and increasing competition from the internet. What are the characteristics of businesses that will thrive in the next generation?

7 What new opportunities does this create for your company and industry in the next 15 years?

Business Owner Interview Questions

1 What made you decide that it was time to exit your business?

2 How did you start the process?

3 How long did it take until you were "clear" of the company?

4 What, if anything, surprised you about the process?

5 Which advisors (professions, not names) were of the greatest value in executing your plan?

6 Were you happy with the result?

7 What did it feel like on your first day as a "former owner?"

8 What was the best thing about exiting?

9 What was the worst thing about exiting?

10 What are you doing now?

GLOSSARY

Exit Planning Terms

A Glossary of Exit Planning Terms

The following is a list of terms used with regards to the exit planning, sale and transfer of a business. It is designed to be a quick reference, not a comprehensive directory.

Baby Boomers	**Generation X**	**Millenialls**
1946 ~ 1964	1965 ~ 1982	1983 ~ 2000

This list, along with many tools, checklists, articles, white papers, and an assessment to help you determine the level of your exit preparedness are all available for free at www.YourExitMap.com.

Appraiser Certifications: There are several organizations that offer professional accreditation programs for business appraisers. Candidates must meet a set of established criteria which demonstrate competency in the field of business appraisals. If you are seeking a valuation of your business, you should make sure that your appraiser holds at least one of the certifications listed below:

ABV: Accredited in Business Valuation
(American Institute of Certified Public Accountants)

ASA: Accredited Senior Appraiser
(American Society of Appraisers)

CBA: Certified Business Appraiser
(Institute of Business Appraisers)

CVA: Certified Valuation Analyst
(American Institute of Certified Public Accountants)

CFA: Chartered Financial Analyst
(CFA Institute)

Baby Boomers: Baby Boomers not only impacted business in America, they remodeled every aspect of society as they passed through it. They were born from 1946 (end of World War II) through 1964. Although slightly exceeded in number by the Millennials, they had an outsized effect on the U.S. economy for over 40 years. They number almost 77 million or about 25% of the population.

Business Brokers: Intermediaries who specialize in the sale of "Main Street" businesses. Typically, a business broker will prepare listing information, advertise, and communicate with prospective buyers. Some may request up front retainers, but the majority of a broker's compensation is usually from a 10% to 12% commission on the sale.

Capital Gains Tax: A lower rate than the tax on ordinary income, utilized on the sale of stock or of assets for which there is a substantial basis. The tax is levied on the profit realized on the sale of a business that was originally purchased at a cost amount that was lower than the amount realized on the sale. An important consideration when structuring a transaction.

Due Diligence: The process of examining all the records and systems of a company before completing a sale. Due diligence typically includes some level of confirmation testing (audit) of financial reports, interviews with key personnel and outside relationships, and a review of all contractual obligations to establish the value of assets and liabilities and evaluate commercial potential.

EBITDA: Earnings before interest, taxes, depreciation and amortization is a cash flow measure that takes into consideration the expenses (interest, depreciation, and amortization) that are deducted as accounting entries from the pretax profits. It is often used as an indicator of a company's financial performance.

Entrepreneurial Buyers: A buyer class that includes individuals or small groups (partners) who are buying or looking to buy a Main Street company in anticipation of working full time to generate a living. This is often seen as a more financially prudent and less risky option than building a company from scratch, because the Main Street business has already been proven to generate paying customers.

ERISA: Employee Retirement Income Security Act of 1974 is the Federal law that establishes the minimum standards and attendant guidelines for tax advantaged retirement savings plans. In order to be funded with pre-tax dollars, an ERISA qualified plan must be open to all employees. (For more information see the U.S. Dept. of Labor ERISA webpage.)

ESOP: An Employee Stock Ownership Plan is a federally regulated method for selling a business to its employees in a manner that is tax-advantaged to both seller and buyer. ESOPs require extensive compliance both during the transaction and ongoing afterwards. Therefore, they are seldom cost effective for Main Street or lower Midmarket companies.

Family Business Office: A professional management team that is dedicated to overseeing one or more wealthy families' investments. In recent years family offices have become more active financial buyers in their search for better returns. The single-family office manages the financial and personal affairs of one wealthy family while a multi-family office offers customized solutions and specialized expertise to several affluent families.

Fair Market Value: The price agreed to between a willing seller and a voluntary buyer when both possess full information about the business and are under no constraints or pressure. The purpose of most business valuations is to try to estimate the Fair Market Value of an entity.

Generation X: The tenth generation born as U.S. citizens which immediately followed the Baby Boomers. Although there is some debate, Gen X is most frequently defined as those born from 1965 through 1982. Sometimes referred to as America's neglected "middle child" because it is a generation bookended by two much larger generations, the Baby Boomers and the Millennials.

Growth Consulting Systems: A documented process for improving the profitability and value of a business. Some of the most popular growth consulting systems include:

EOS: The Entrepreneurial Operating System, created by Gino Wickman and outlined in the book *Traction*, is a system that seems to work especially well in smaller companies who have never used an organized planning system.

Gazelles: A comprehensive system of online forms and support outlined in Verne Harnish's new book *Scaling Up*. Gazelles is an excellent system for fast-growing companies, technology based businesses, and those who seek to outgrow the neutral zone.

VBS: The Value Builder System process grew out of John Warrillow's book *Built to Sell*. This approach is more focused on business metrics rather than the personal objectives focus of exit planning, but many exit planners include VBS as part of their offerings.

Investment Bankers: Bankers that work for financial institutions in the business of raising capital for companies, government and other entities. They act as intermediaries in the sale of mid-market businesses. While Investment Bankers raise capital, they more often search out qualified buyers and arrange controlled auctions.

LBO: A Leveraged Buyout is the purchase of a company by using its own balance sheet to finance (leverage) the purchase. The assets of the company being acquired are often used as collateral for the loans. It is a frequent methodology used by managers to buyout an owner.

Long Term Installment Sale: After the value of a company is agreed upon, at least one employee agrees to purchase it and promises to pay the agreed-upon amount. The owner holds a promissory note with installment payments over a seven to ten year period, signed by the buyers. The note is secured by the assets and stock of the business and the personal guarantee and collateral (usually residences) of the buyers. Little or no money is paid at closing.

M&A: "Mergers and acquistions" is the overarching term for all activity surrounding the buying and selling of businesses, although it is more commonly associated with larger transactions. A merger means combining two companies to form a new company, while an acquisition is the purchase of one company by another in which no new company is formed.

Main Street: The common term for companies with valuations and selling prices up to $3,000,000. They are what most people think of when discussing "small business," an operation where the owner(s) are completely involved with day to day functional responsibilities. Main Street businesses are usually sold to entrepreneurial individuals who are seeking full time employment as an owner.

Midmarket: Companies that are valued between $3,000,000 and $50,000,000, or between Main Street businesses and large M&A interests. They generally have between fifty and a thousand employees. The middle market represents a significant part of the U.S. economy with one-third of private sector GDP employing approximately 25% of the total labor force.

Millennials: : Persons born after Generation X, from 1983 through 2000. They are also sometimes referred to as Generation Y. They are the first to have come of age in the new Millennium. Millennials now number 80 million, surpassing the 77 million Baby Boomers (ages 51-69). Young immigrants have also been a factor in adding to the numbers of Millennials in the U.S.

Modified Buyout: This method utilizes the concept of discounted stock value combined with tax favored payments including deferred compensation, consulting fees, real estate lease payments, qualified retirement plan contribution increases, etc. The idea is to make the transition affordable for the buyer yet maximize the value received by the seller. It is a two part plan and most banks will finance this type of purchase.

Neutral Zone: Companies whose value is too great to be affordable to an individual buyer, but who aren't sufficiently profitable to attract financial investors. Too big to be small and too small to be big, these businesses have typically between $5M and $10M in gross revenue with a Fair Market Value between $3M and $5M. They usually realize less than $1M in pretax profit.

NQDC: Non-Qualified Deferred Compensation plans are defined as any non-ERISA compliant compensation plan that is inherently discriminatory regarding eligibility. It can be either an elective or non-elective plan, agreement, method, or arrangement between an employer and an employee to pay the employee compensation in the future. For example, stock options for C-level executives.

PEGS: Private Equity Groups are investment partnerships whose primary focus is the purchase and sale of businesses exclusively to produce returns for their investors. Selling to a PEG may be a great exit strategy for an owner who wants or needs to get substantial liquidity out of the business but also desires to remain in operational control.

Quality of Earnings Audits: A specialized due diligence audit most commonly used by PEGS. Its purpose is to discount earnings (and the resultant purchase price multiple) by identifying customer concentration or competitive risks, along with unrecognized liabilities such as employees' accrued vacation time.

SBA: The U.S. Small Business Administration provides support to entrepreneurs and small business. It is a government-backed guarantor of banks' small business loans. The SBA does not lend money, but rather insures the primary lender via either its 504 (real estate) or 7A (business value) programs.

SDE: Seller's Discretionary Earnings is a Main Street approach to valuation determined by the total financial benefit derived from an owner's compensation and other company-paid benefits. It includes pretax and pre-interest profits before non-cash expenses, the owner's benefits, and non-related income or expenses.

Strategic Buyers: A class of buyers considered an M&A level purchaser who buys a business for specific, differentiable products, services, technical knowledge, intellectual capital or contractual relationships. Their goal is to identify companies whose products or services can synergistically integrate with their existing P/L to create long-term shareholder value.

USPAP: The Uniform Standards of Professional Appraisal Practice is the national organization that disseminates ethical performance valuation standards for all other certifications. Compliance is required for state-licensed and state-certified appraisers.

Virtual Equity: Any of a variety of plans (e.g. phantom stock, equity appreciation rights), intended to retain and reward key employees. These plans are typically characterized by awards based on organizational value, and qualifications for payouts over a lengthy time period or conditional on a change in ownership. They are by definition Non-Qualified Deferred Compensation.

Picture Index

Pages v, xiii, 1, 4, 5, 19, 26, 28, 33, 37, 42, 45, 53, 62, 65, 71, 72, 73, 77, 78, 80, 81, 84, 89, 97, 98, 104, 105, 106, 107, 112, 115, 118, 119, 120, 122, 126, 127, 135, 143, 144, 146, 148, 150, 151, 152, 153, 159, 160, 162, 167, 169, 172, 174, 175, 177, 180, 184, 187, 190, 196, 201, 205, 207, 213 / © Copyright 2017 MPN Incorporated.

Pages xiii, 1, 3, 7, 8, 10, 13, 14, 16, 19, 24, 25, 26, 28, 29, 30, 33, 35, 37, 38, 39, 41, 42, 45, 46, 47, 48, 49, 50, 51, 53, 55, 56, 58, 59, 60, 61, 62, 64, 68, 82, 83, 85, 87, 89, 91, 92, 93, 94, 96, 97, 100, 101, 102, 103, 108, 109, 110, 114, 117, 121, 122, 124, 125, 126, 127, 128, 129, 130, 131, 132, 135, 137, 138, 139, 140, 143, 147, 149, 150, 154, 155, 156, 157, 158, 162, 164, 166, 168, 171, 174, 175, 176, 177, 178, 179, 181, 182, 183, 186, 189, 191, 193, 201, 213 / © Images used under license from Adobe Stock.

Pages 17, 21, 31, 35, 40, 53, 58, 60, 64, 66, 68, 69, 71, 73, 76, 77, 80, 81, 82, 83, 85, 105, 116, 117, 121, 125, 143, 153, 154, 156, 164, 166, 167, 194, 195/ © Images used under common reuse license from Shutterstock.

Page 4 / © Image used under common reuse license from Good Free Photos.

Pages 6, 9, 10, 11, 12, 13, 14, 17, 18, 20, 22, 23, 24, 36, 38, 44, 57, 75, 86, 94, 124, 138, 141, 142, 163, 198, 215 / © Images used under common reuse license from Wikimedia.

Pages 6, 46, 138 / © Images used under common reuse license from Wikipedia.

Pages 9, 11, 12, 15, 29, 44, 46, 48, 66, 69, 70, 72, 74, 75, 215 / © Images used under common reuse license from Flickr.

Pages 11, 38, 41, 72, 77, 124, 170, 175, 194 / © Images used under common reuse license from Pixabay.